Drawing Dogs:

Using Zen Doodle Technique
Step by Step Guide

By Jeremy Knowles

Copyright©2016 Jeremy Knowles

Table of Contents

Disclaimer

While all attempts have been made to verify the information provided in this book, the author does assume any responsibility for errors, omissions, or contrary interpretations of the subject matter contained within. The information provided in this book is for educational and entertainment purposes only. The reader is responsible for his or her own actions and the author does not accept any responsibilities for any liabilities or damages, real or perceived, resulting from the use of this information.

The trademarks that are used are without any consent, and the publication of the trademark is without permission or backing by the trademark owner. All trademarks and brands within this book are for clarifying purposes only and are the owned by the owners themselves, not affiliated with this document.

Introduction

Dogs are an important part of our lives. Often, they are thought of as members of our families. It is believed that the modern day dog evolved from a wolf-like ancestor some 40,000 years ago. Since that time, they have been bred for specific characteristics and physical attributes. Some of the things we use dogs for include herding, hunting, protecting our homes, assisting handicapped people, pulling loads and assisting police and military officials.

Dogs show more variety in their characteristics due to breeding than any other kind of domesticated animal. They have very keen senses of hearing and smell with their sense of sight much less developed. They vary in size from the English Mastiff, which can be as much as 98 inches long to the Yorkshire Terrier, which is only about four inches in length. On average, dogs live from about ten to thirteen years or more.

Studies have shown that mixed breeds tend to live longer than purebred dogs and that the heavier the weight of a dog, the shorter the lifespan. Most dogs reach sexual maturity anywhere from six months to about a year. Smaller breeds tend to have smaller litters (an average of about six) and larger breeds tend to have more (twelve or more).

Dogs vary greatly according to their breeding. Dogs such as Labradors and huskies are working dogs, which are bred to assist humans with specific tasks such as retrieving game and pulling heavy loads, in these cases. The temperament of dogs such as this tends to be loyal, hardworking, and energetic. The size and shape of a dog often reflects its breeding and the purpose it was bred for. For example, dachshunds were originally bred to go into burrows after animals such as badgers. Other dogs, such as the Pomeranian are bred more for their appearance and less for practical purposes, although even the Pomeranian was descended from a working dog called a Spitz.

The Zen doodle technique that is being used in this book is very easy to make your own. Anyone who has ever been bored and scribbled on a piece of paper has designed a doodle. The technique is all about creating a variety of patterns that are combined together in one drawing. You mark a specific shape or region and then begin to fill that region with a specific pattern such as concentric circles, floral designs or any type of repeating shape or pattern.

The 'Zen' aspect refers to the state of our minds when we draw and doodle, which is very similar to a meditative or 'Zen' state of mind. Once you've gained experience using this technique, you will be able to have the various patterns fit together as a whole within the context of the features of an animal or person. So, if you love dogs; and you would like to practice the use of the Zen doodle technique, this is the book for you.

Chapter 1 – German Shepard

These dogs are very loyal to their owners. German shepherds sometimes have a reputation for being vicious guard dogs; but they can also be loving and devoted members of the family.

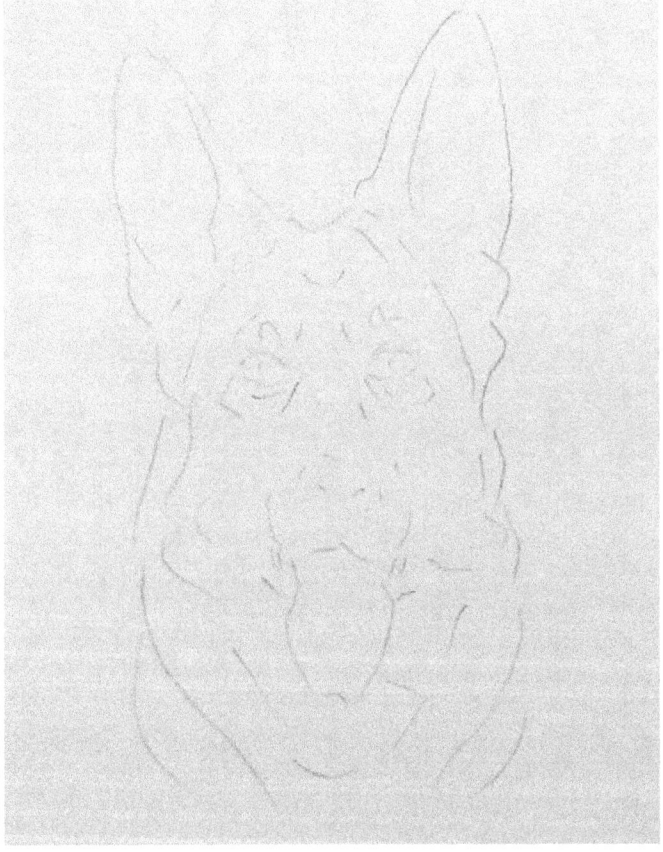

Make the faint outline of the dog's head with triangular ears. Draw in the dog's eyes as small ovals, including the short marks underneath it. Draw the nose and mouth and subtle marks that make up the folds in its neck and the edges of its face. Beneath the nose, make a shape thatwill be the dog's tongue.

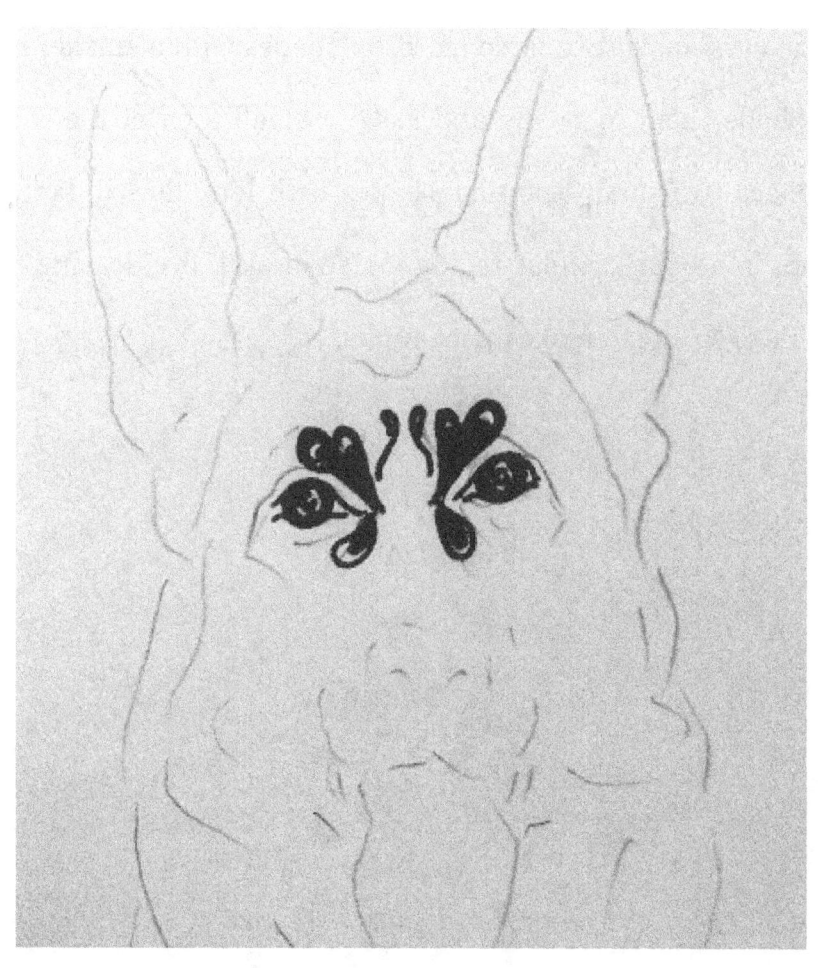

Around the eyes, make two large teardrop shapes with a smaller one below the two. Shade them in boldly and leave a small area at the top without shading. Place two small bean-like shapes with long tails in between both eyes. Shade in a bold, circular region inside of each eye, leaving a small 'c' shape inside each one to make up its pupils.

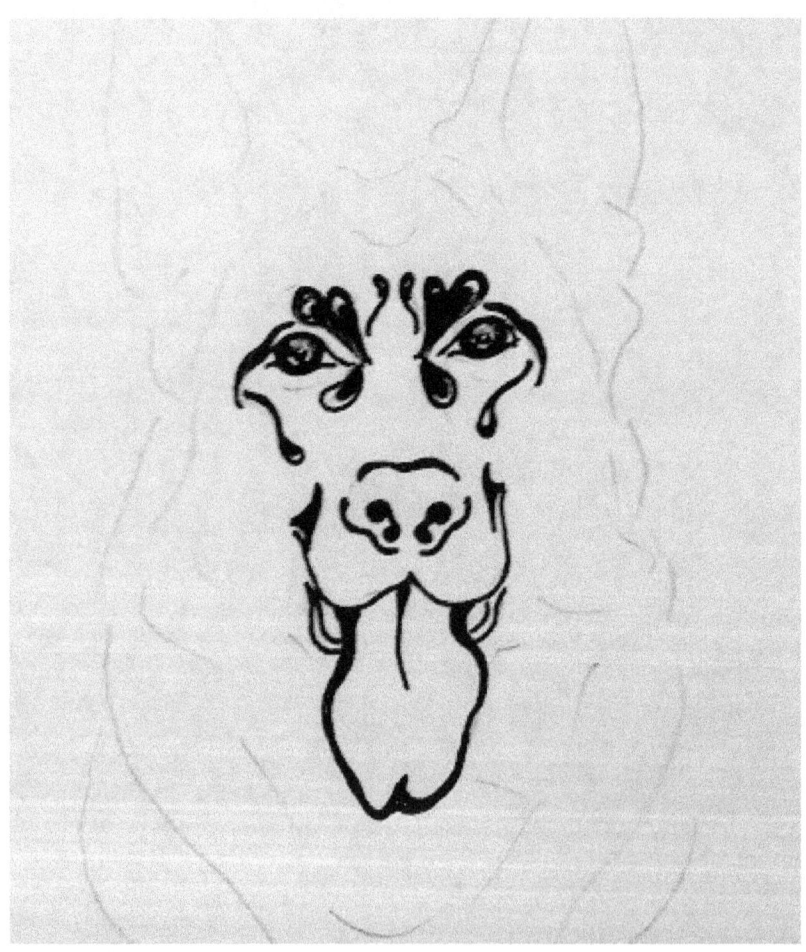

Add two more teardrop shapes with tails below each eye, leaving a small area at the end unshaded. Go over the nose and mouth with darker shading. Make sure to add thicker areas of shading on either side of the nose, on the nostrils; and along the edges of the tongue.

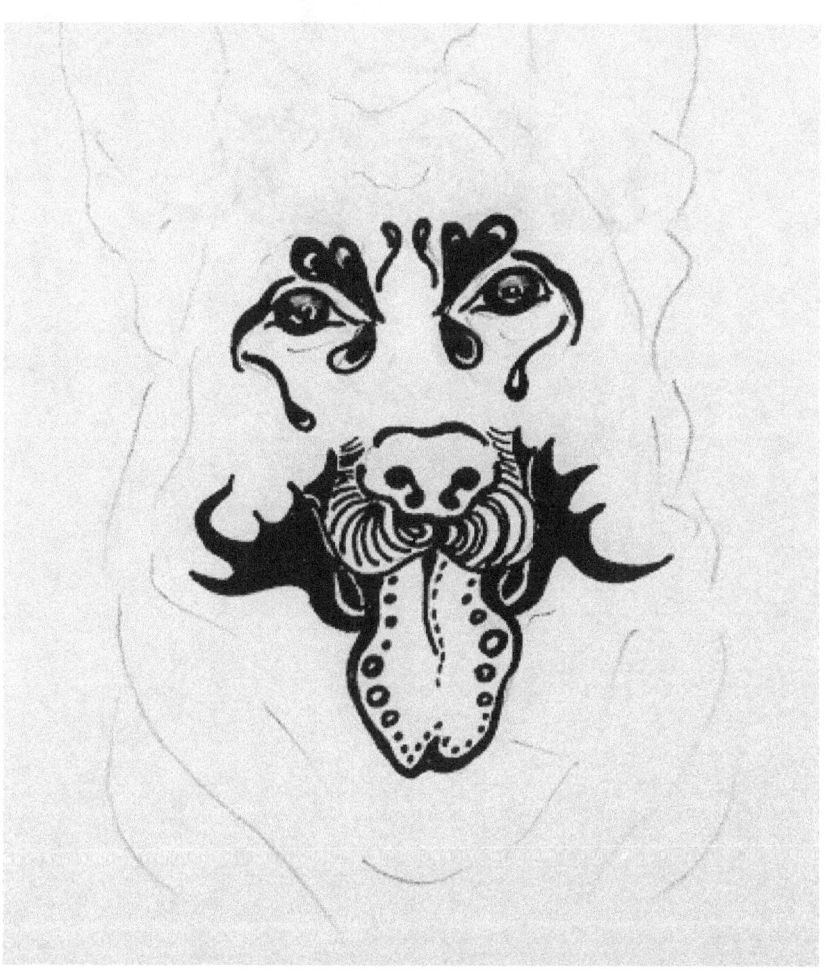

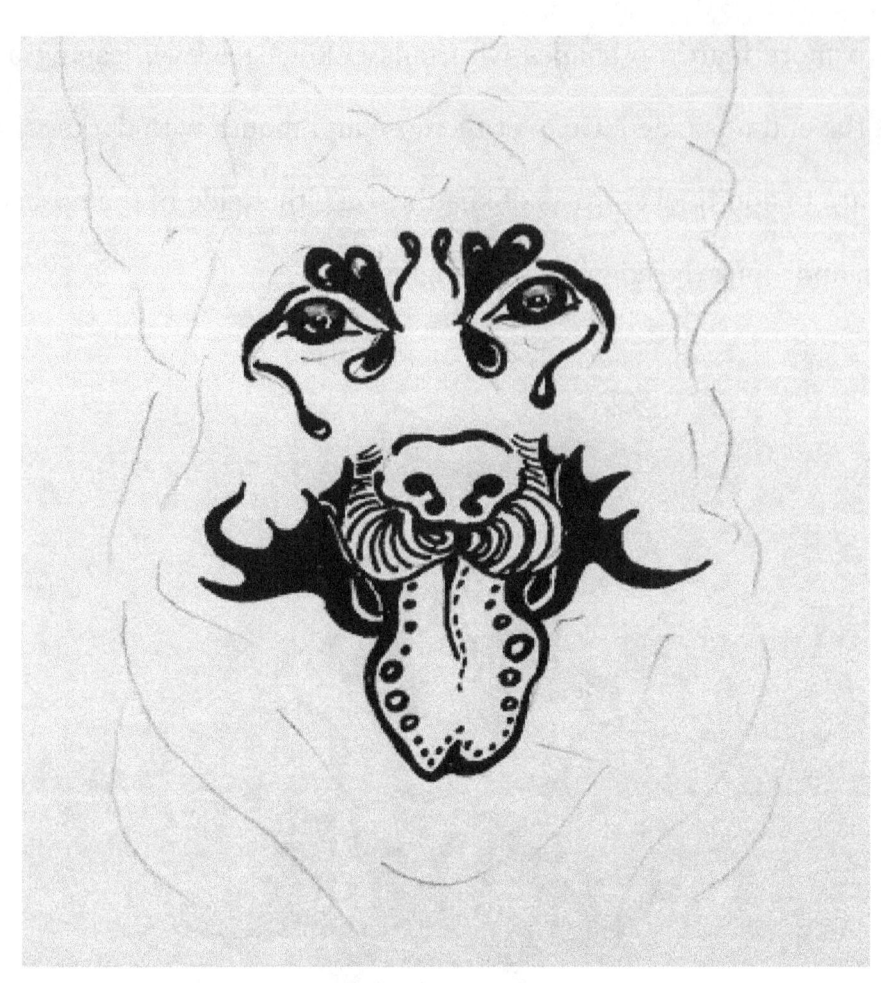

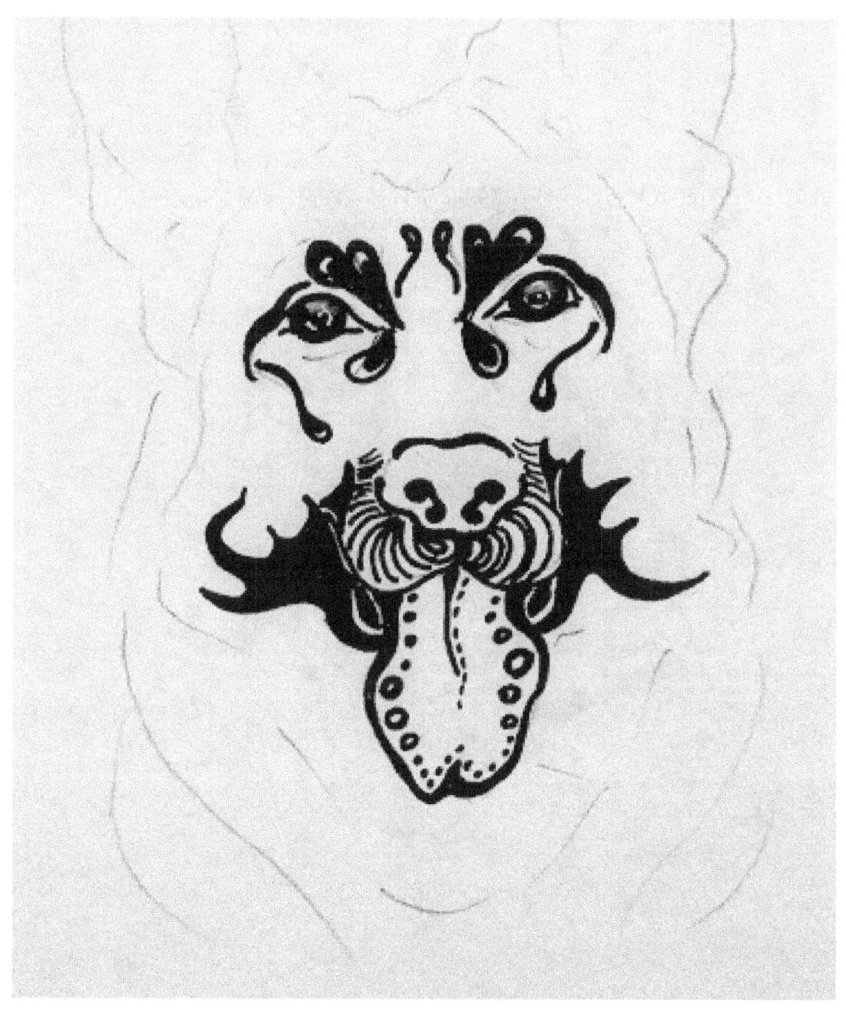

In the regions below the nose, add several concentric, curved lines that are very small at the top and larger beneath the nostrils. On either side of the nose/mouth region, make the large shaded area shown in the drawing with several points along it. On the tongue, make a series of small circles along the edges.

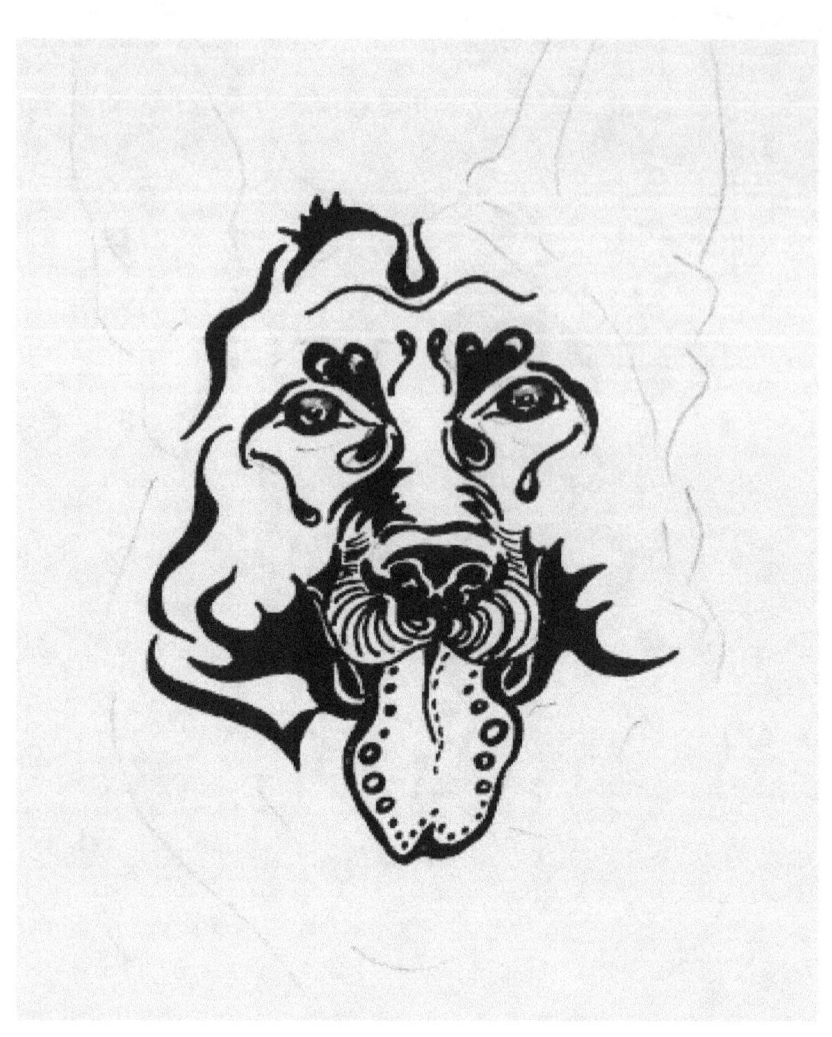

On the left side of its face, make a shaded, curved, V-shape that curves upwards. Above this mark, make another shaded, curved shape. Then, draw a third shaded, curved shape on the upper left portion of the dog's face. Make another pointed, shaded region that curved inwards on the forehead. Below the curved area, make an 'm' shaped line. Now, make a shaded, zig-zag region between the eyes and nose. Shade in the region above and between both nostrils.

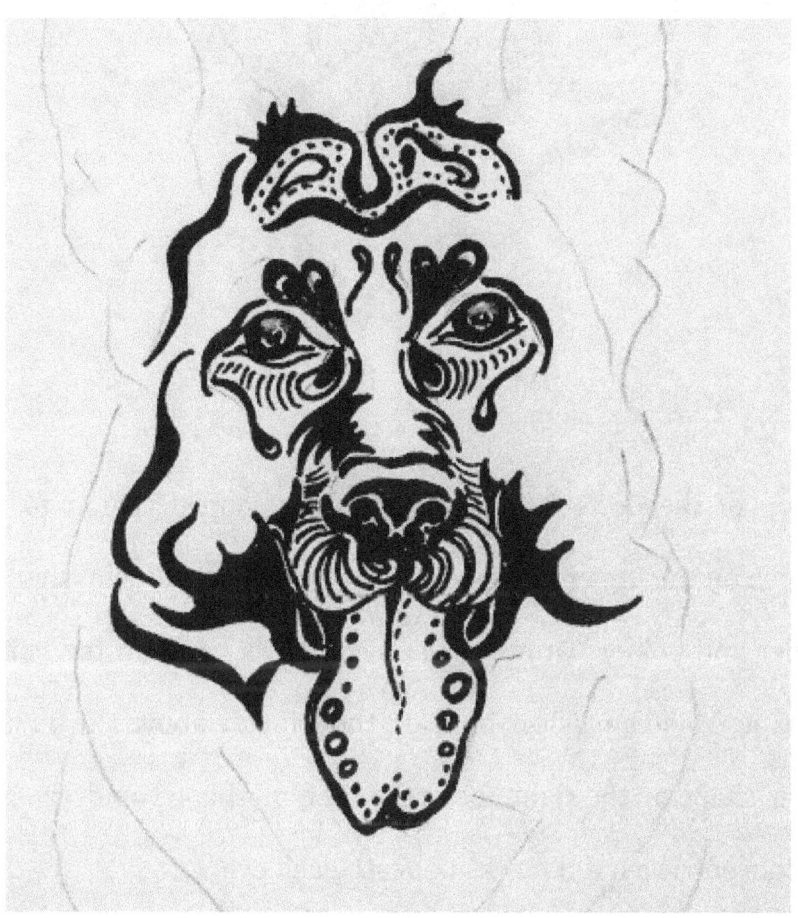

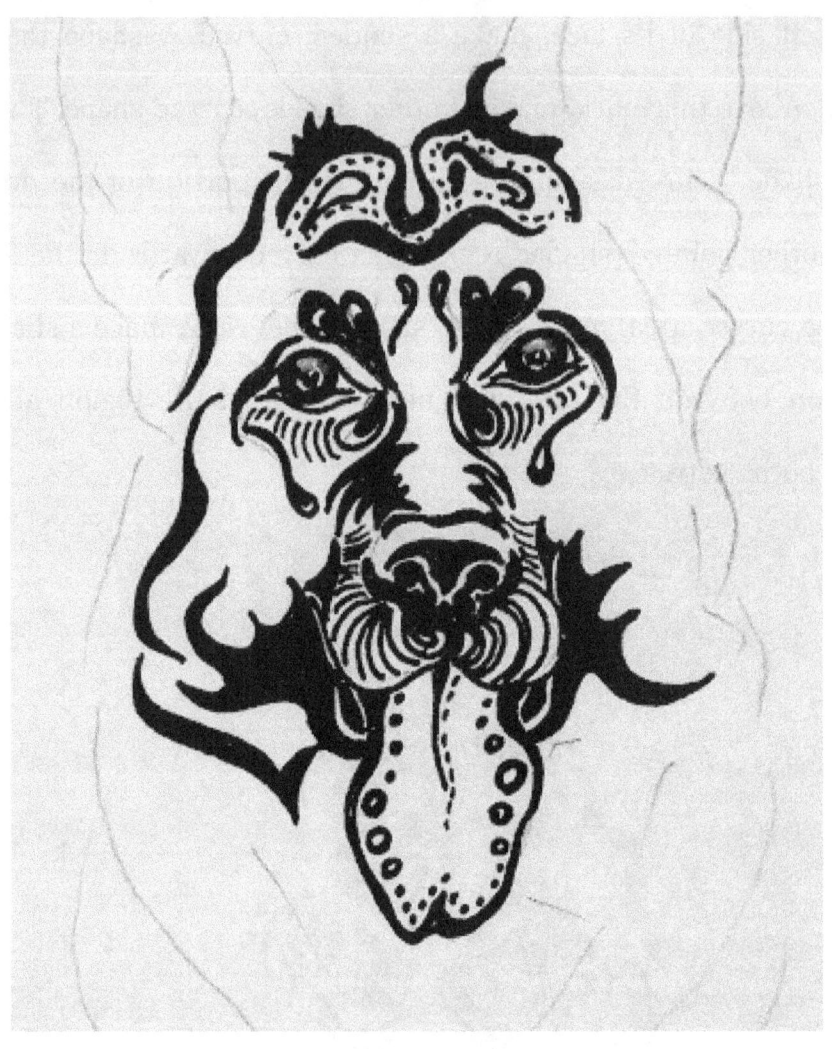

On the top of the dog's head, add onto the looped region to make the pointed area on the upper right side of its head. Make the 'm' shape beneath this heavier and bolder. Draw in a series of dots between the very top and the 'm' shape. Make a paisley shape on the left side above the 'm' shape and another 'm' shape on the right above the first 'm' shape you drew. Now add a series of concentric curved marks beneath each eye.

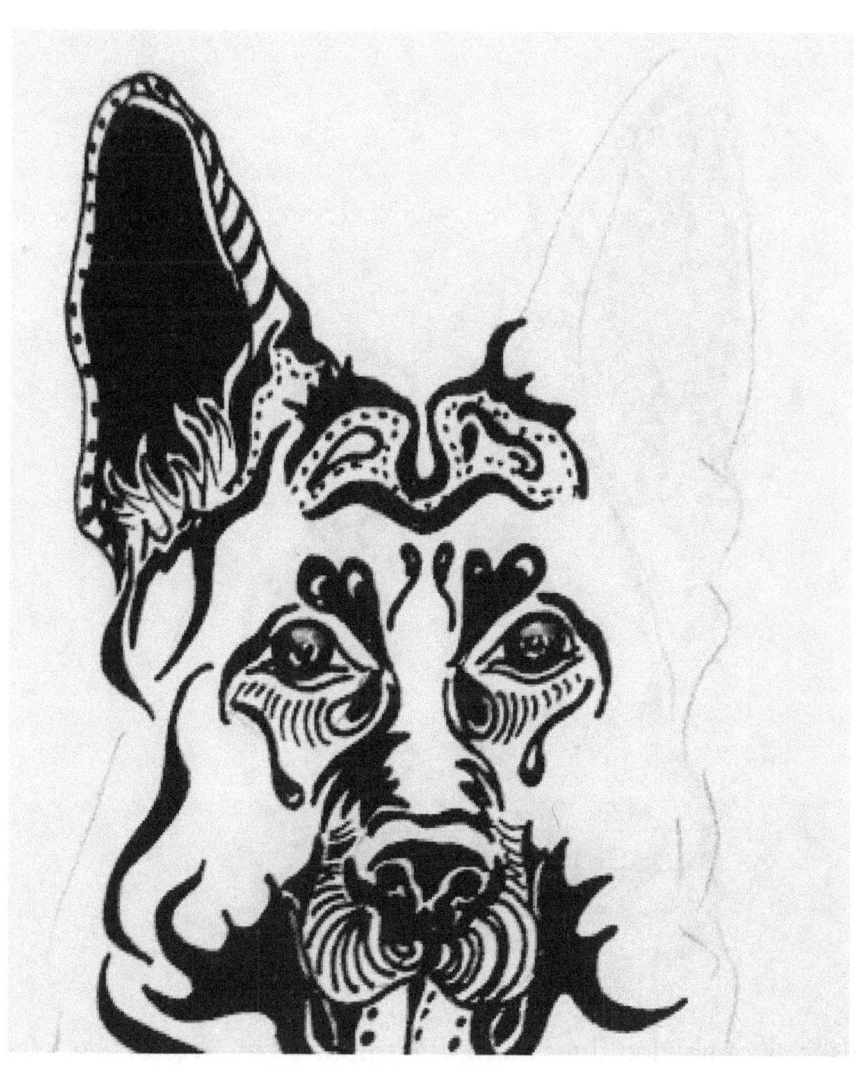

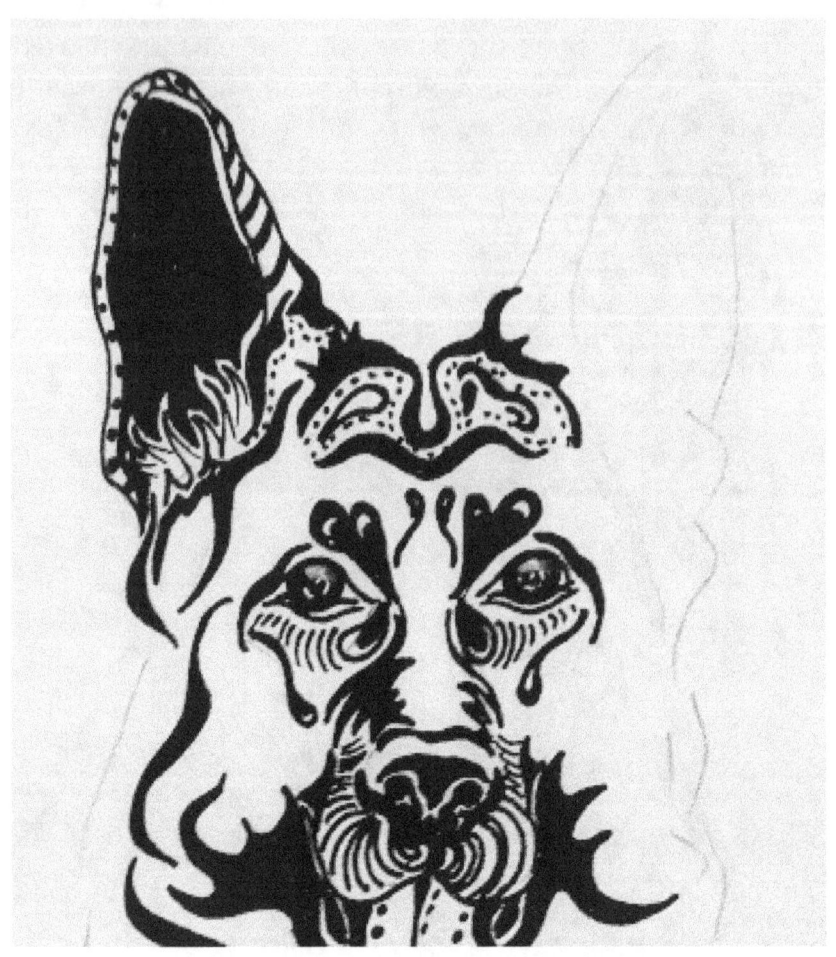

Make a series of shaded lines along the upper right edge of the left ear and make smaller bold marks along the left edge of the ear. Shade in the middle of the ear boldly. Beneath the ear, make a series of flame-like shapes. Add some small dots along the lower right portion of the ear.

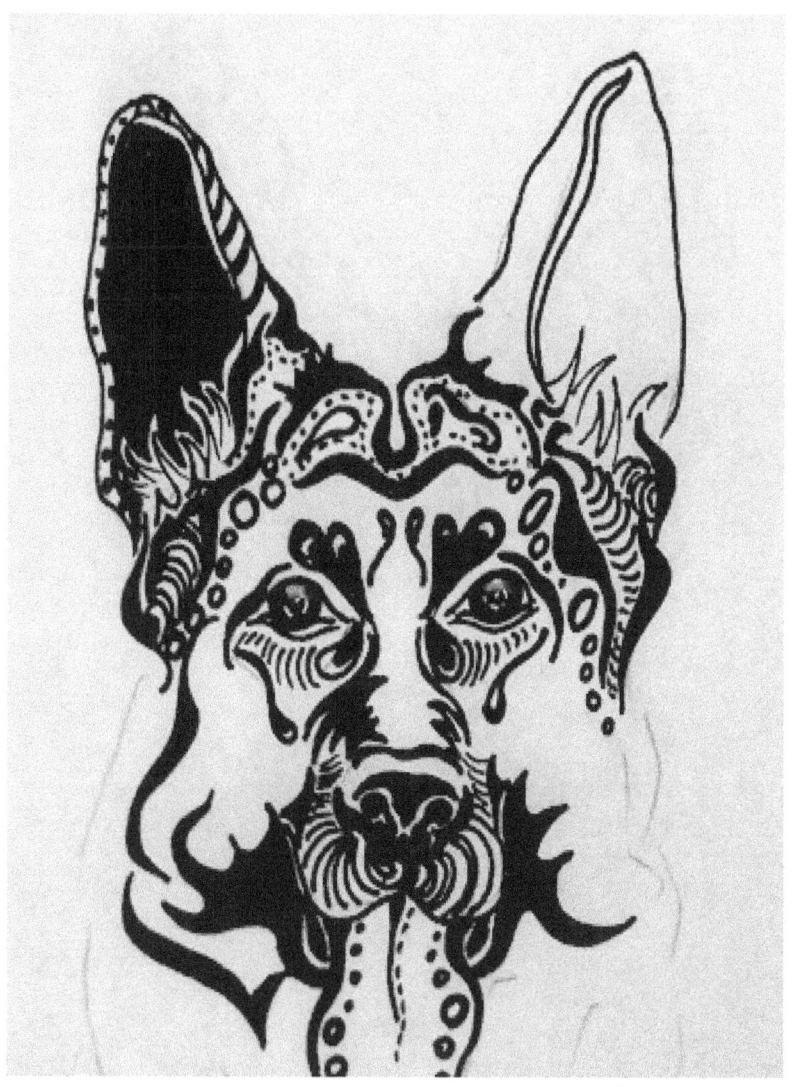

Make a series of concentric lines below the flame-like shapes you made. Now add a series of circles that extend diagonally below the right and left ears. Add some flame-like shapes to the dog's right ear and the shaded and concentric curve marks below the flame-like shapes as shown in the drawing.

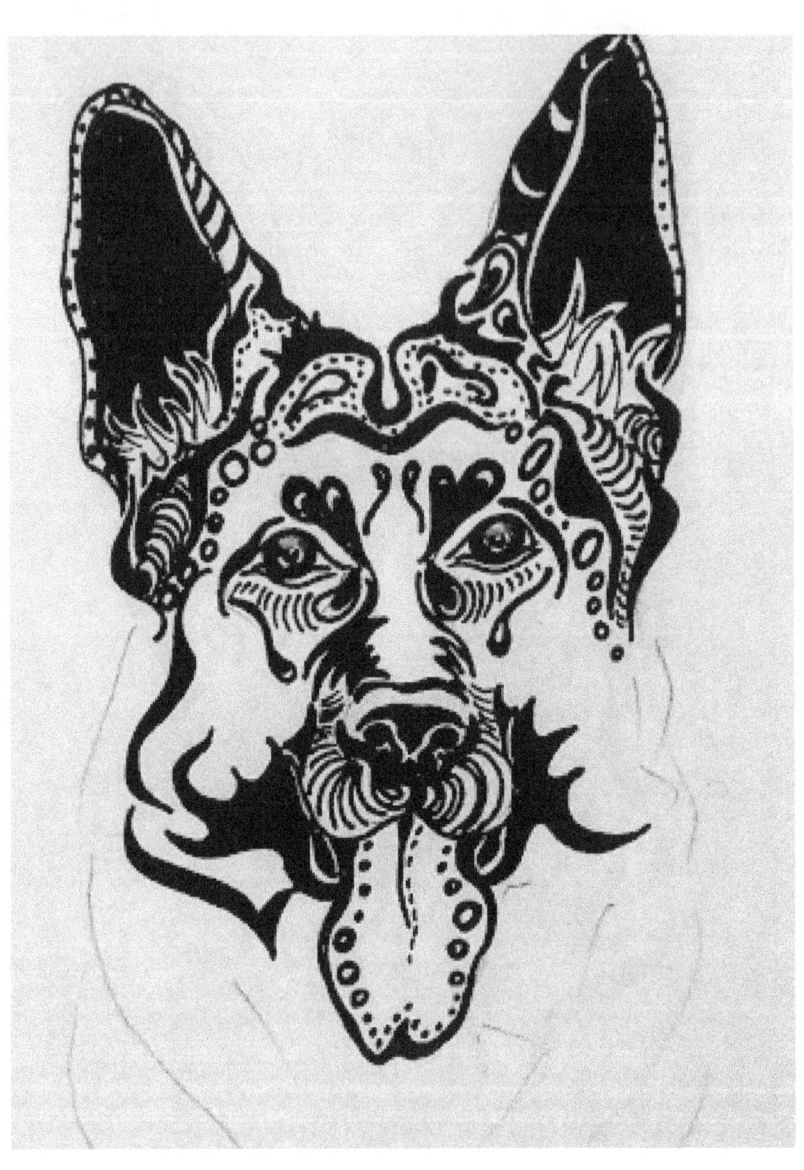

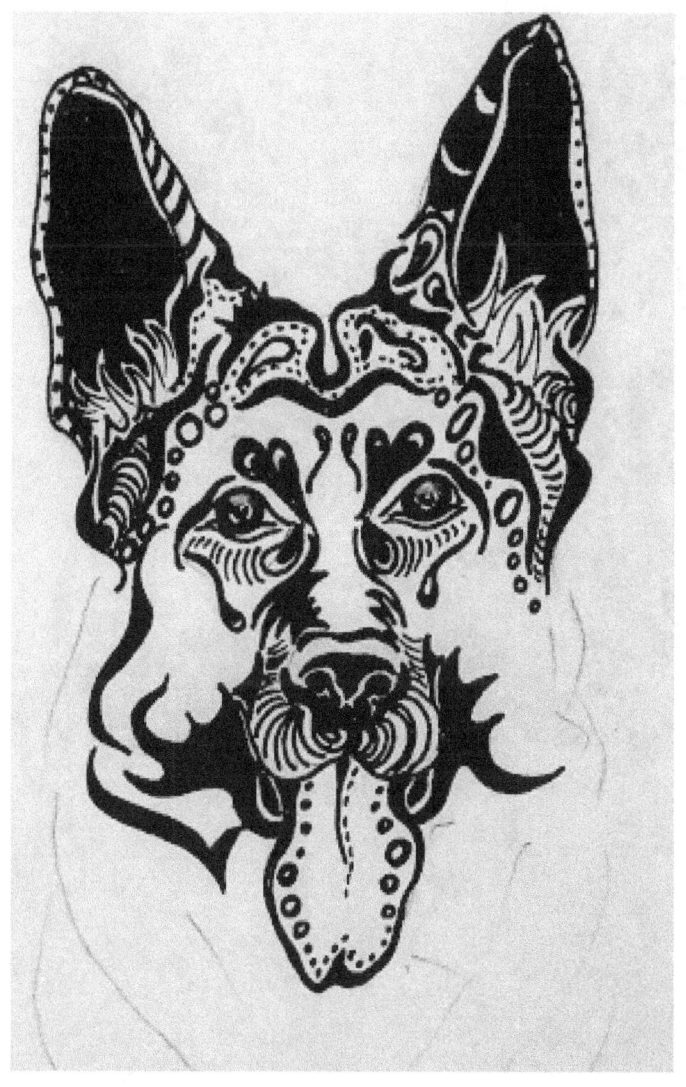

Now, shade in the middle portion of the right ear, leaving an unshaded area around this shaded region. Add some small dots on the right side of the left ear. On the left side of this ear, draw in some lines that will be left unshaded. Shade in the area around these marks. Draw in a couple of tear-drop shapes on the lower left portion of the right ear.

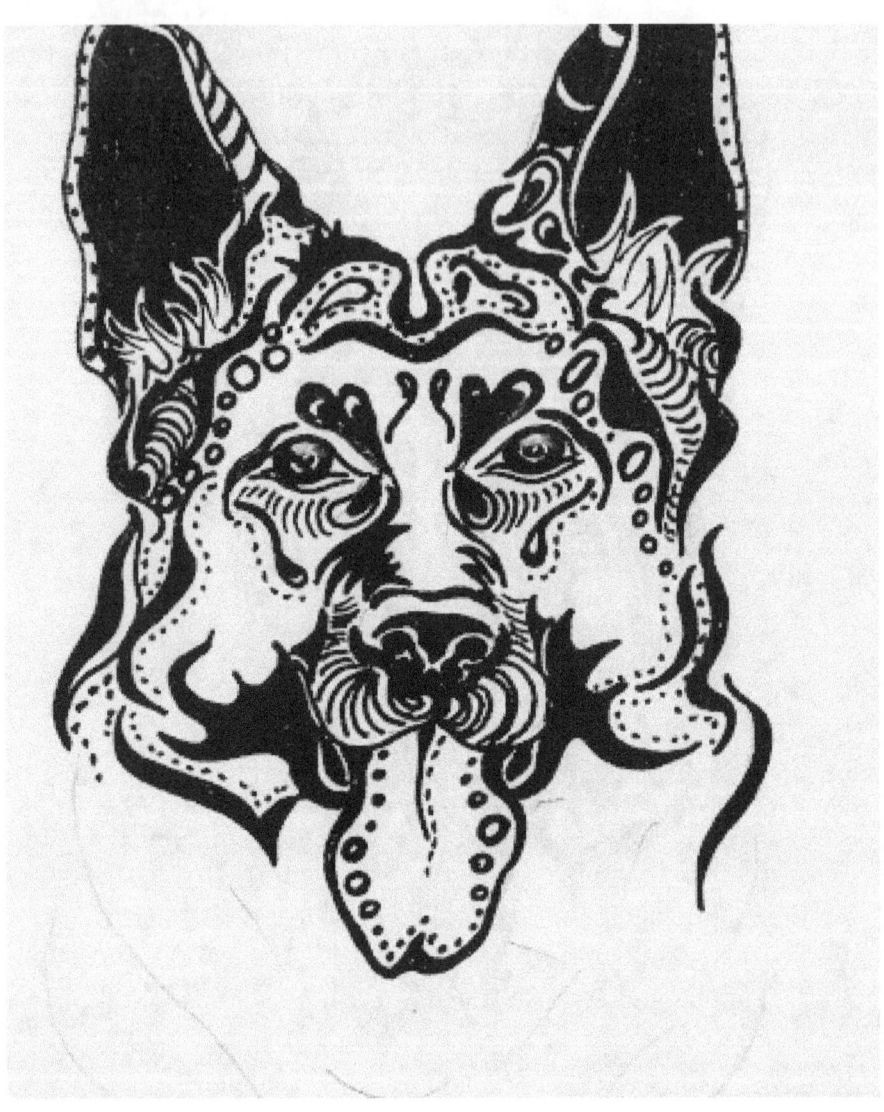

Add in several dotted lines on the right and left portions of the face and beneath the teardrops beneath the eyes. Add in the bold, curved lines along the outside, lower portion of the face.

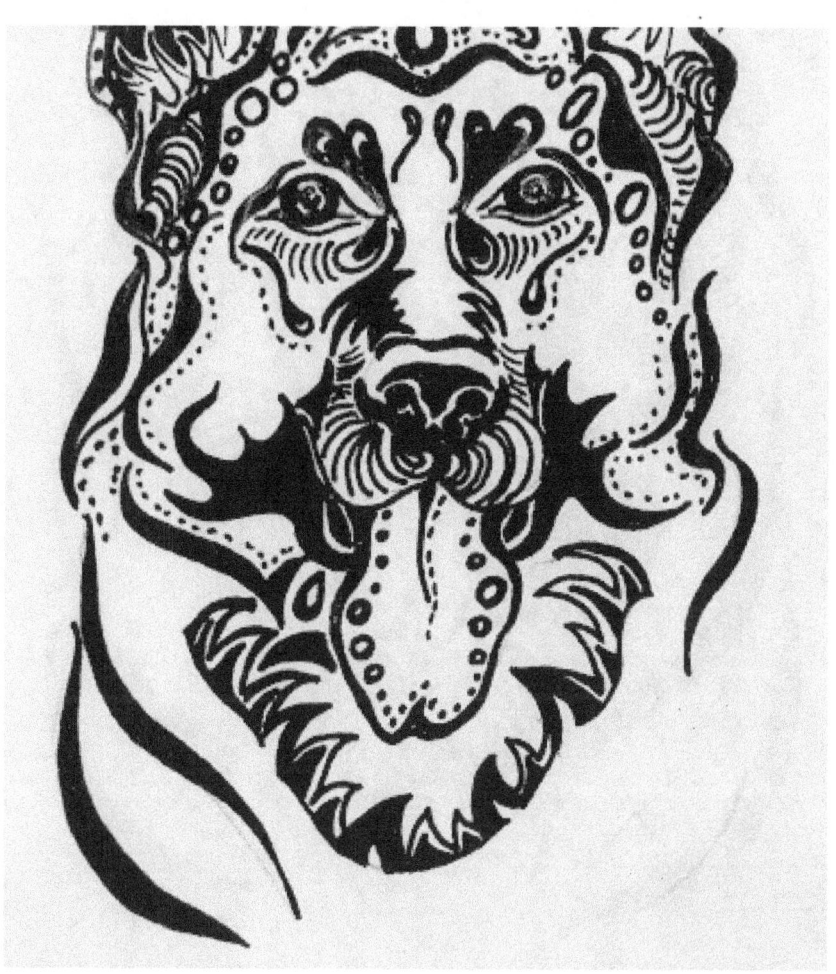

Add two large, bold curved lines on the lower left portion of the drawing. Beneath the tongue, add in the triangular, flame-like shapes that extend from one side of the face to the other. Be sure to copy the pattern, which shows some triangles being shaded on the outside and some on the inside.

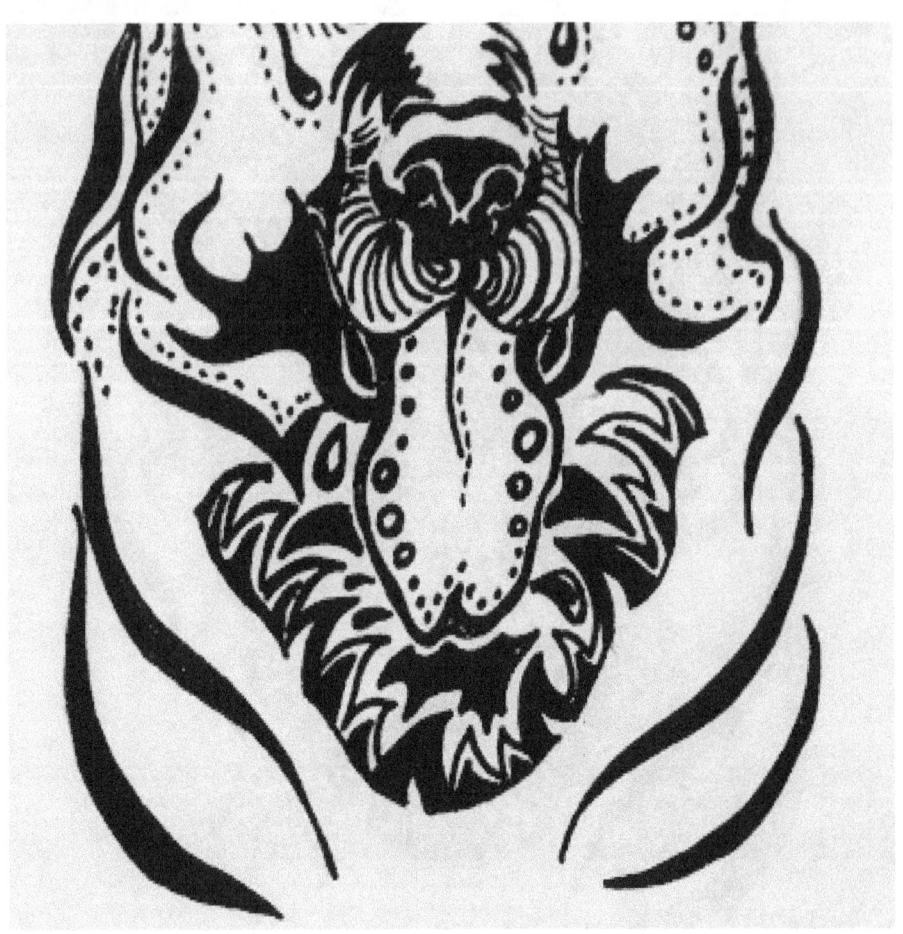

On the lower right side of the drawing, add in two longer, curved lines. In between the tongue and the triangular shapes, add in the irregular, shaded shapes as indicated in the drawing.

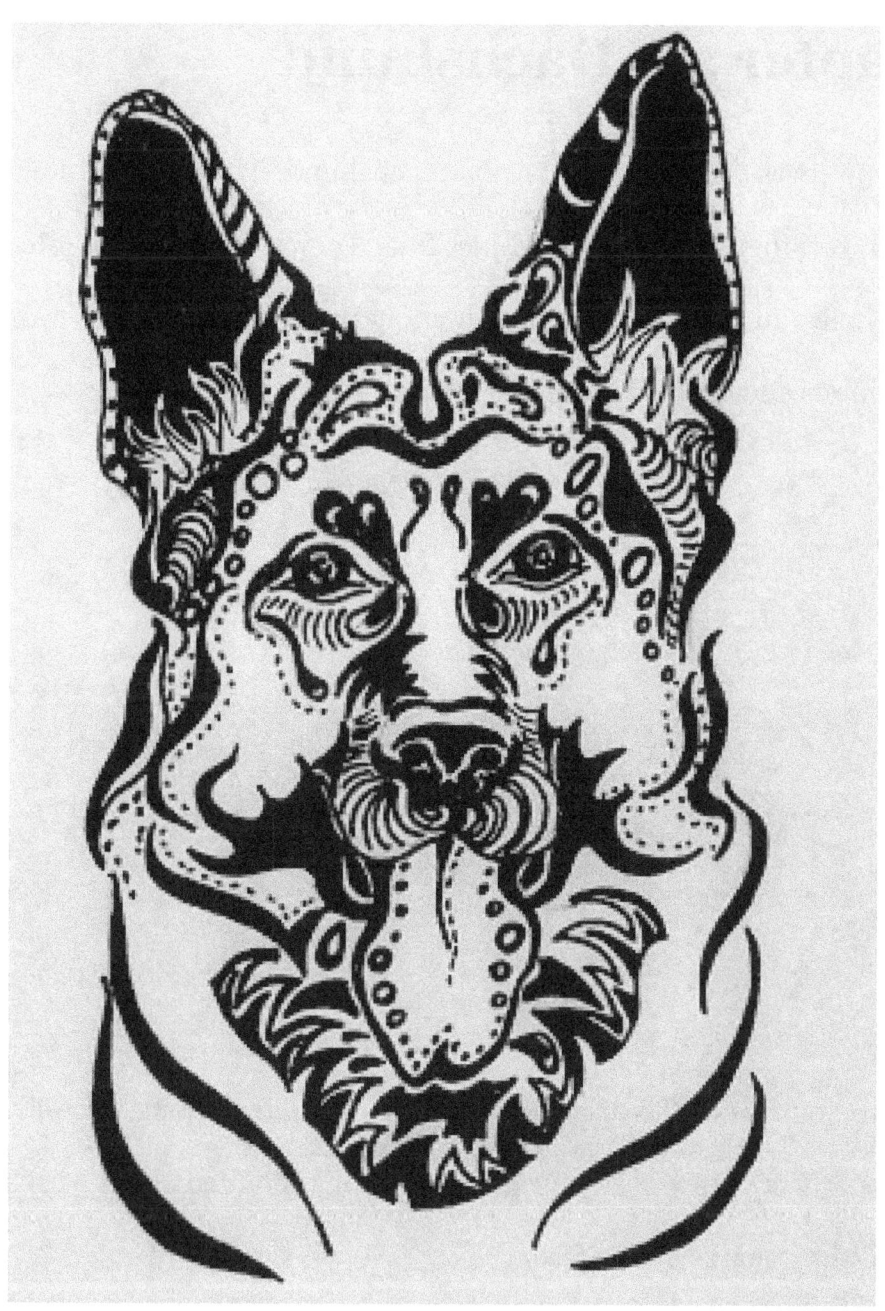

Now here is a look at the completed drawing. Be sure to look over the details and try and fill in any that you may have missed!

Chapter 2 – Dachshund

Everyone loves the long and lovable dachshund. They may be low to the ground; but they can get around just fine. They were originally bred to go down holes in search of a hunter's quarry. Now, they are wonderful companions and devoted family members!

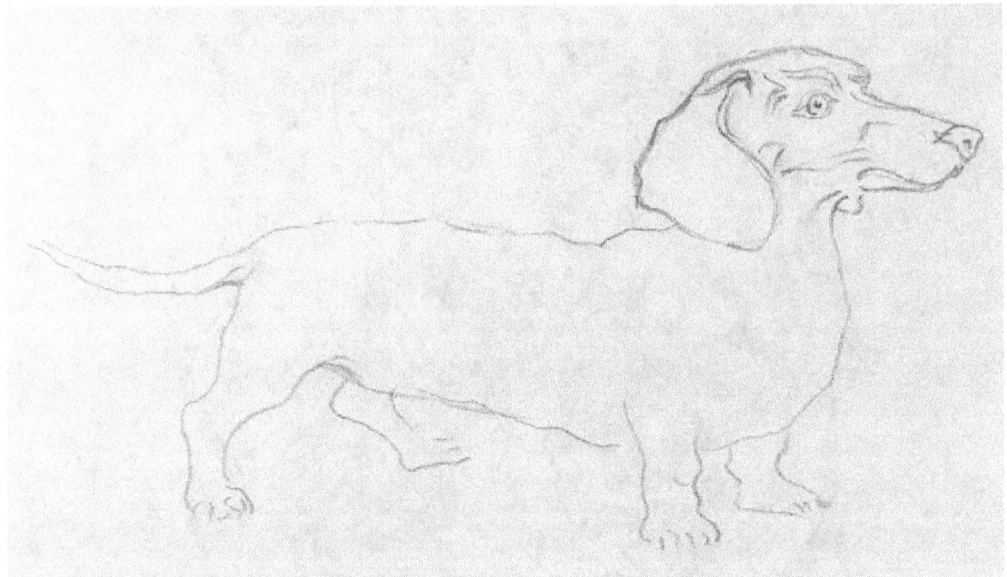

Make the outline of the dachshund's body, including a long, tube-like body with short feet. Draw in floppy ears and a long, pointed snout with a small eye and short marks on the face.

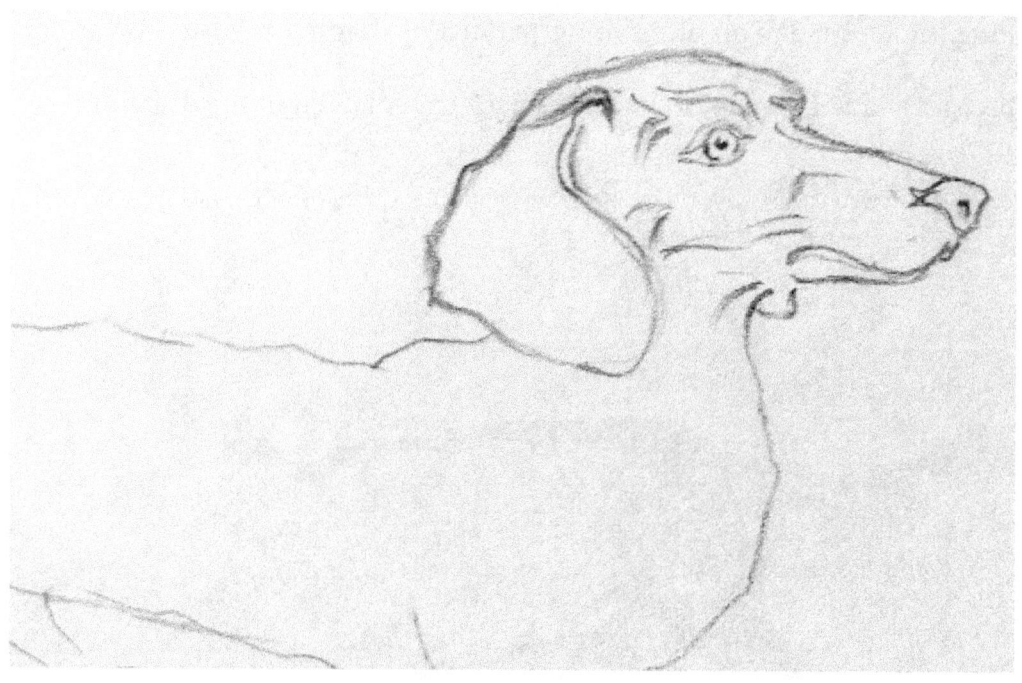

Check to make sure you have included all of the distinguishing marks around the eye, both above and below it.

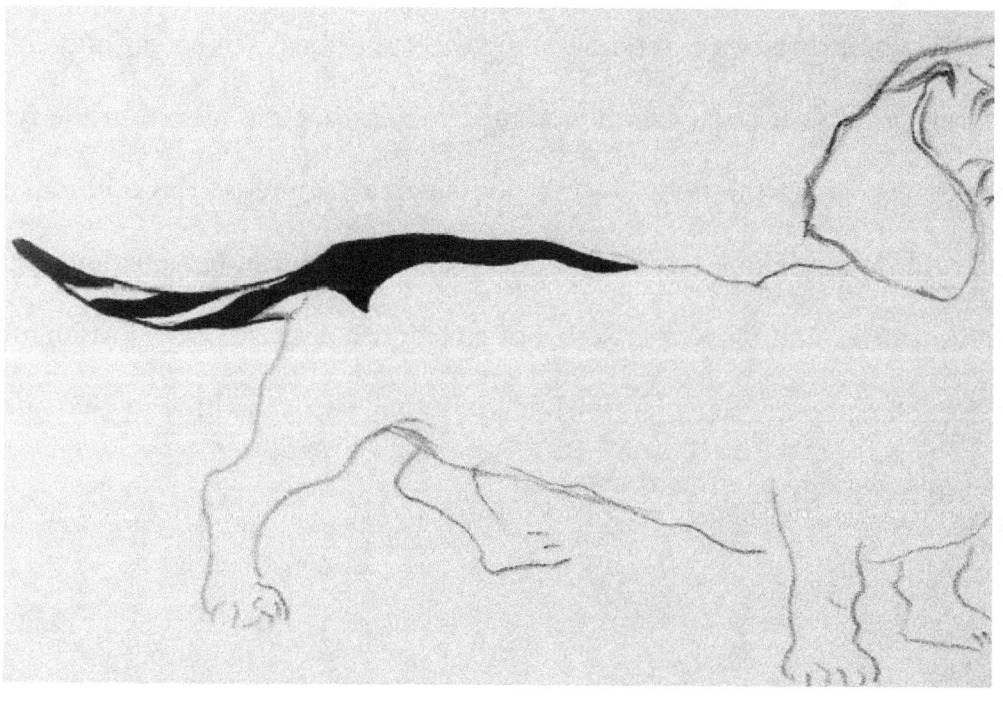

Along the tail, make an alternating pattern of shading followed by a region that isn't shaded. Shade in the upper back as indicated in the drawing.

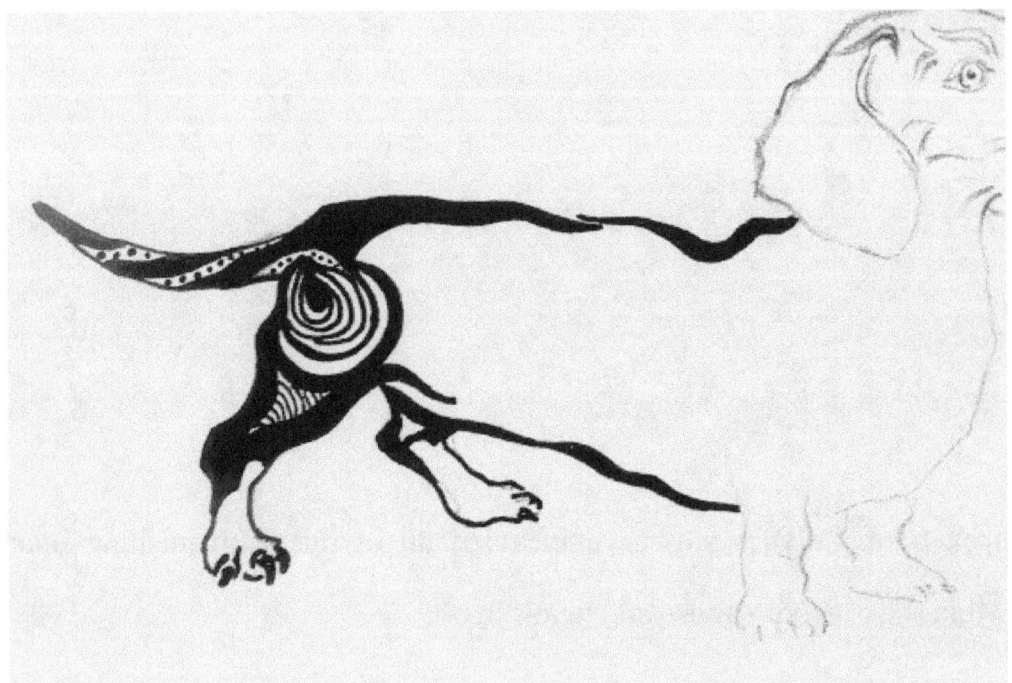

Shade in more regions extending along the upper back to the ear and along the rear, right leg. Draw another shaded region that extends from the rear, left leg and along the belly. In the non-shaded regions of the tail, make a series of dots. Make a circular, shaded region on the upper portion of the rear, right leg and draw in a series of concentric circles. Leave a triangular region on the rear, right leg unshaded so that you can draw in the small, curved lines shown in the drawing.

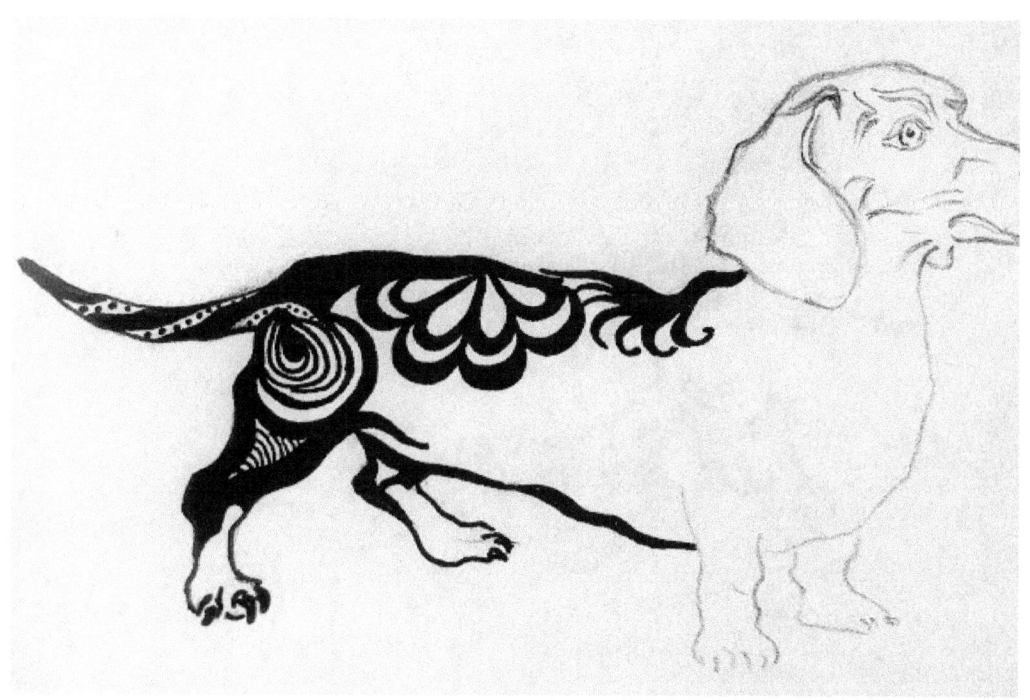

On the dog's upper back, make a series of four teardrop shapes and shade around these. Beneath the region you just shaded, make four, moon-like shapes and shade in the areas beneath these. In the region between the teardrops and the ear, make a series of curved lines that increase their curvature as you move to the right.

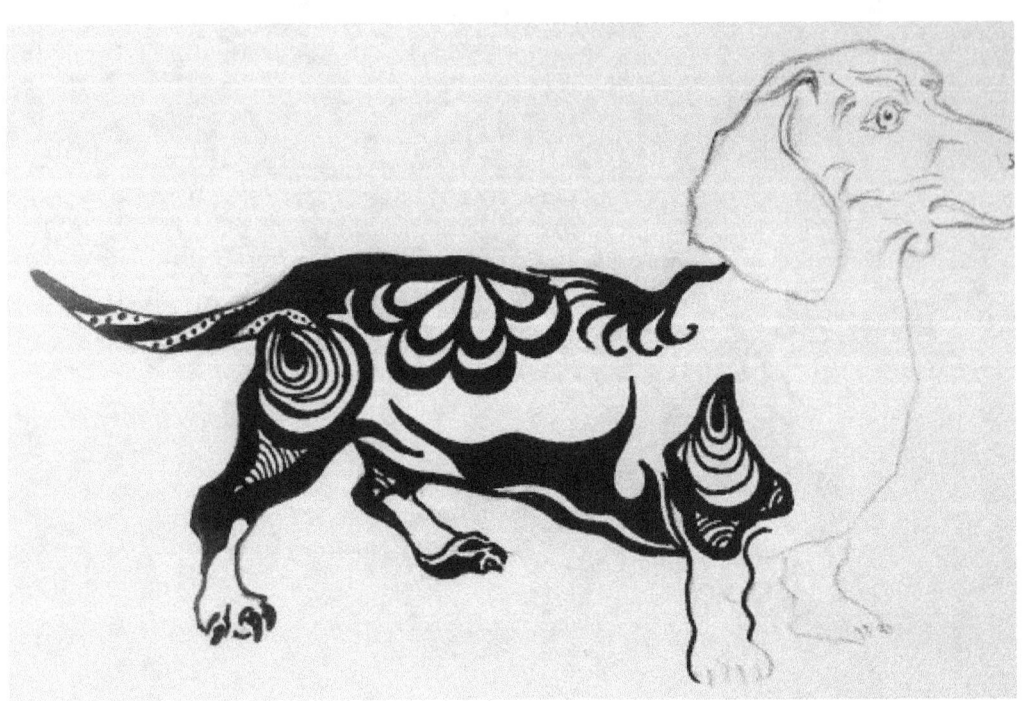

Make a large, irregular shape on the belly region of the dog. To the right of this, make a large, irregular shape with concentric, circular lines within it. Make two regions of lines that are closer together on the bottom portion of this irregular shape. Add the shaded areas shown in the drawing on the rear, left leg and begin to outline the front, right leg boldly.

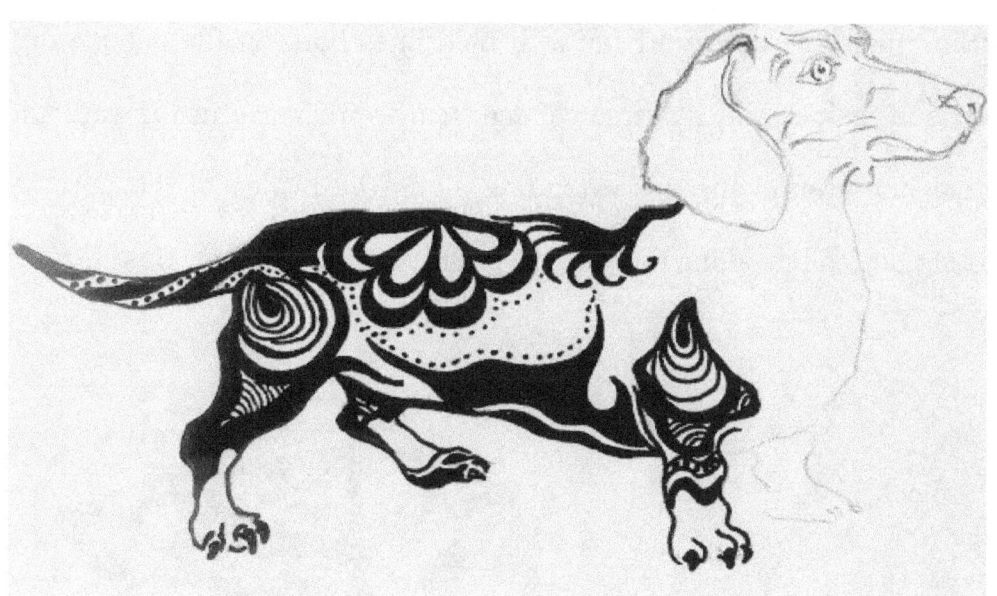

Add in the dotted lines in the middle portion of the body. On the upper, right leg, go over the claws with bold marks and make the curved lines on the upper right leg as shown in the drawing.

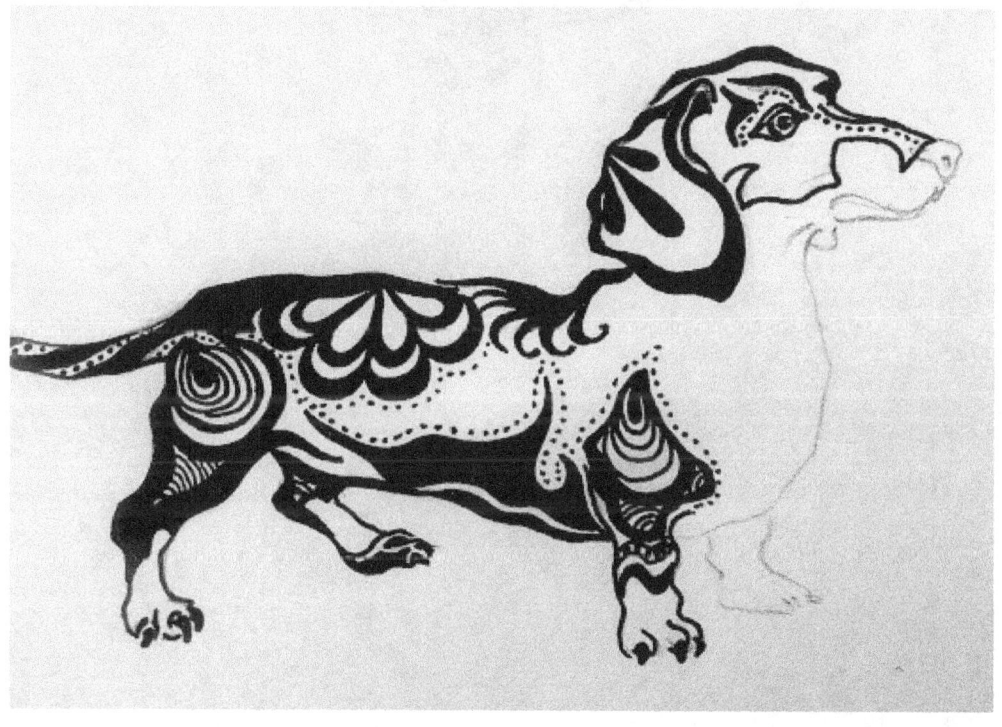

Outline the dog's head and ear with bold lines both on the outside of the head and inside. Add in three shaded, teardrop shapes in the ear. Add a dotted line around the eye extending along the bridge of the nose. Add another dotted line along the irregular shape above the front, right leg.

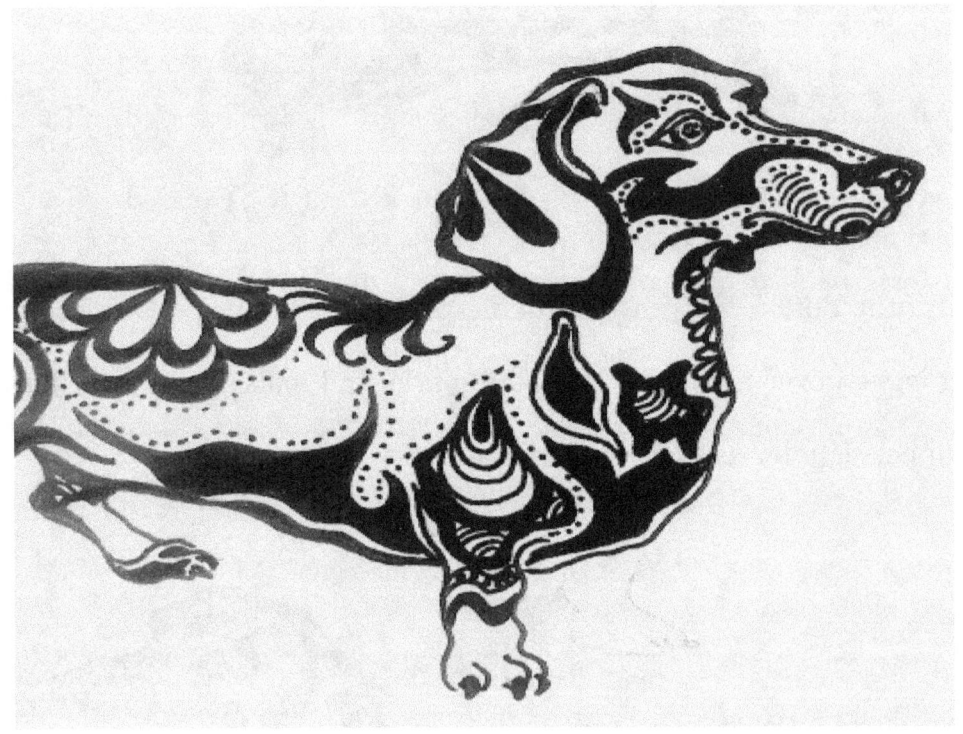

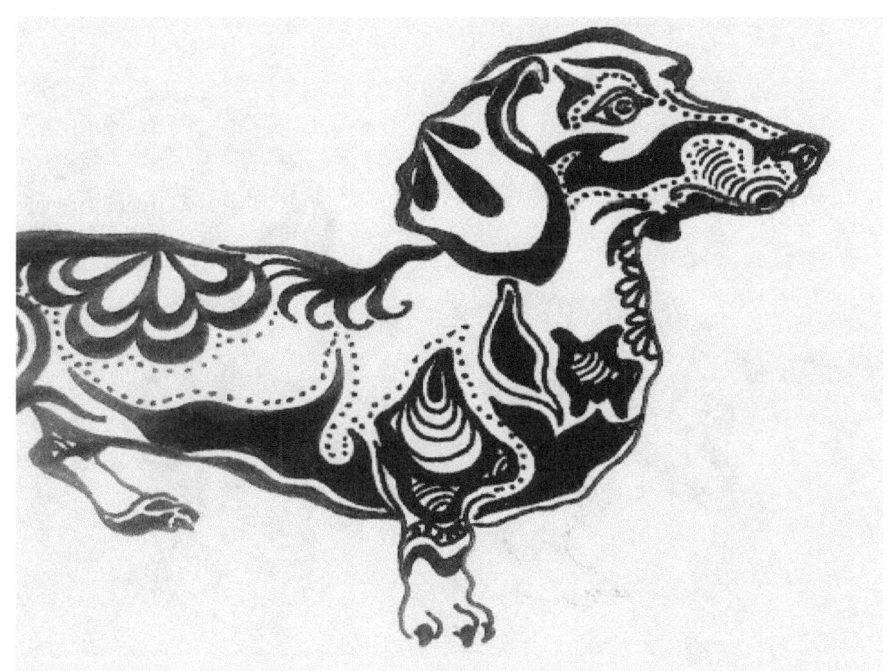

Add in bold, irregular shapes on the front of the dog's body and along the region below the eye. Below the shaded region beneath the eye, make another long, dotted line and add a series of concentric curved marks that extend along the mouth. Add a floral pattern along the right side of the neck.

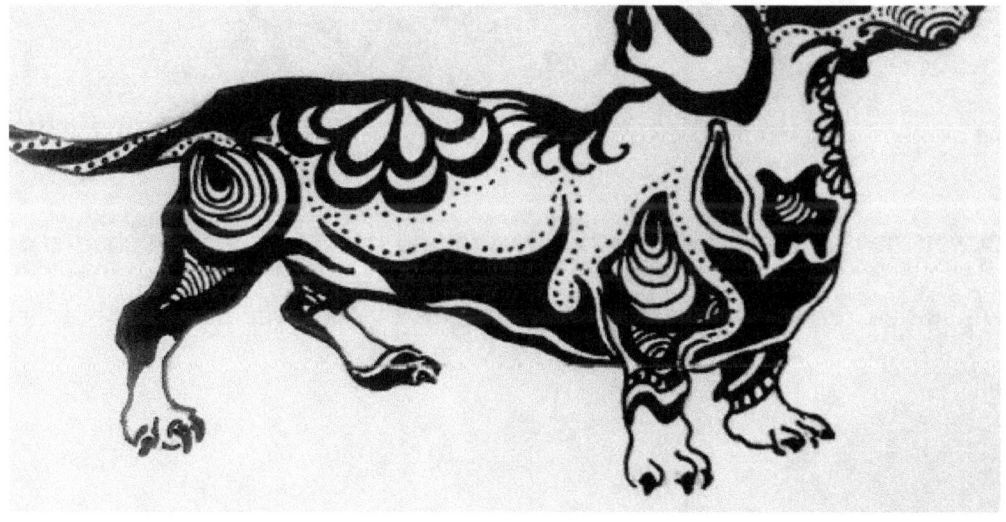

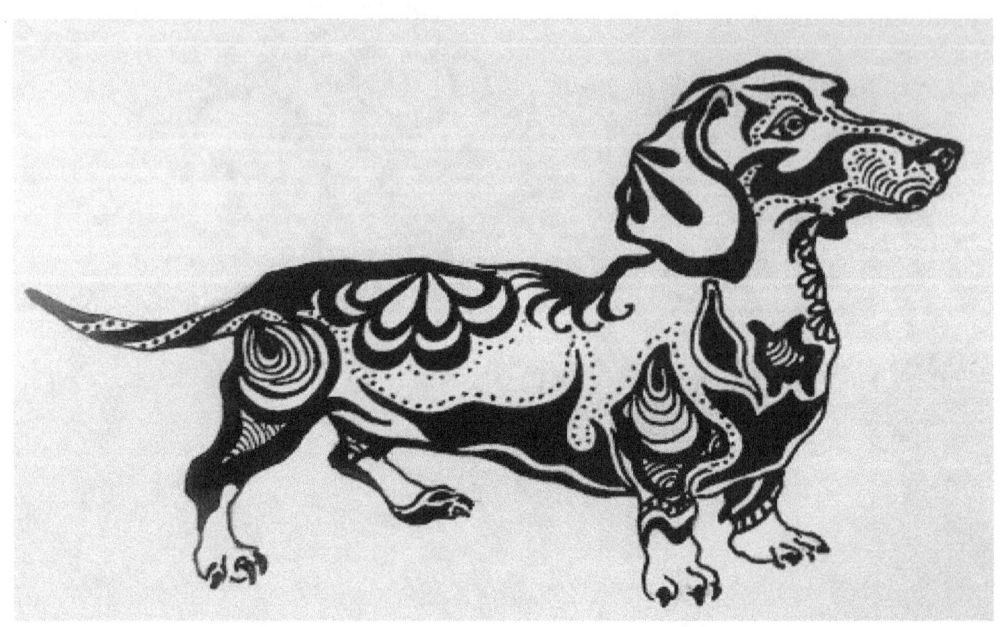

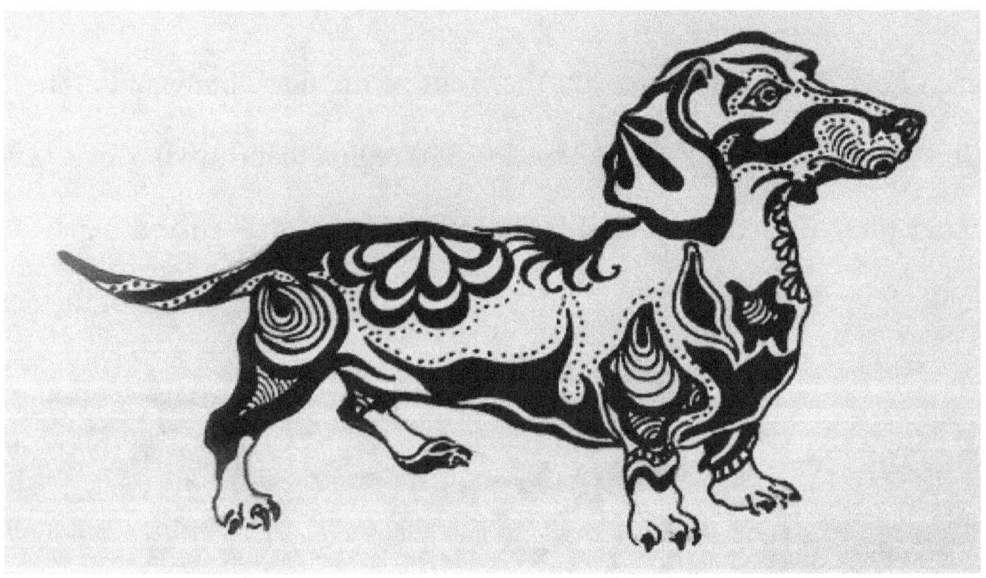

Go over the dog's front, left leg boldly and add in the alternating shaded and non-shaded regions along this leg. Make sure to go over the nails boldly as well.

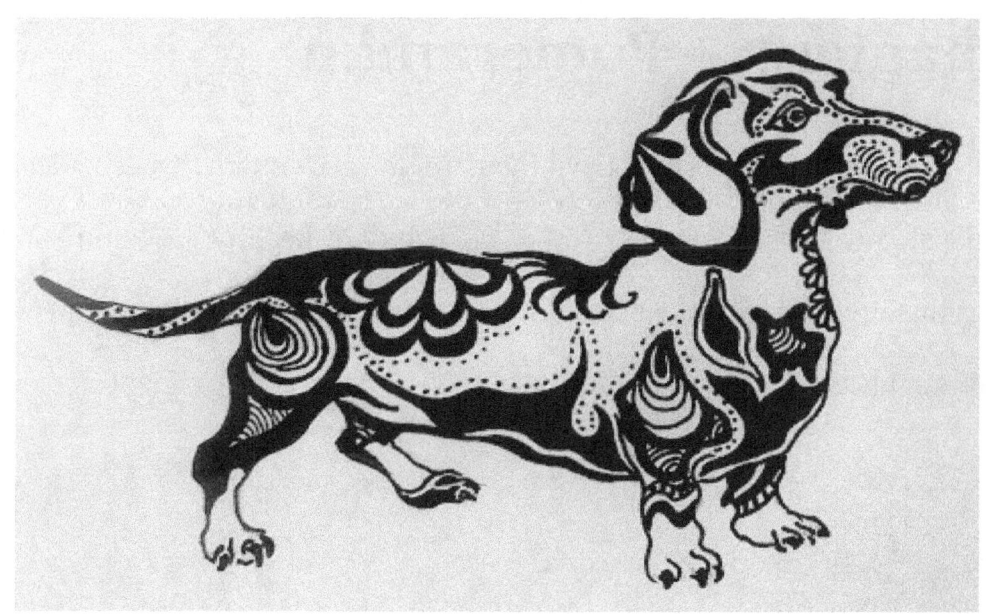

Here is a full view of the completed dachshund! Look over the drawing carefully to make sure there is nothing that you may have left out with the detail.

Chapter 3 – Pomeranian

These adorable balls of fluff have their origin in Germany. Queen Victoria famously owned one of these toy dogs. They are healthy and sturdy little dogs that are sure to find a place in your heart. They are usually very playful, lively and friendly!

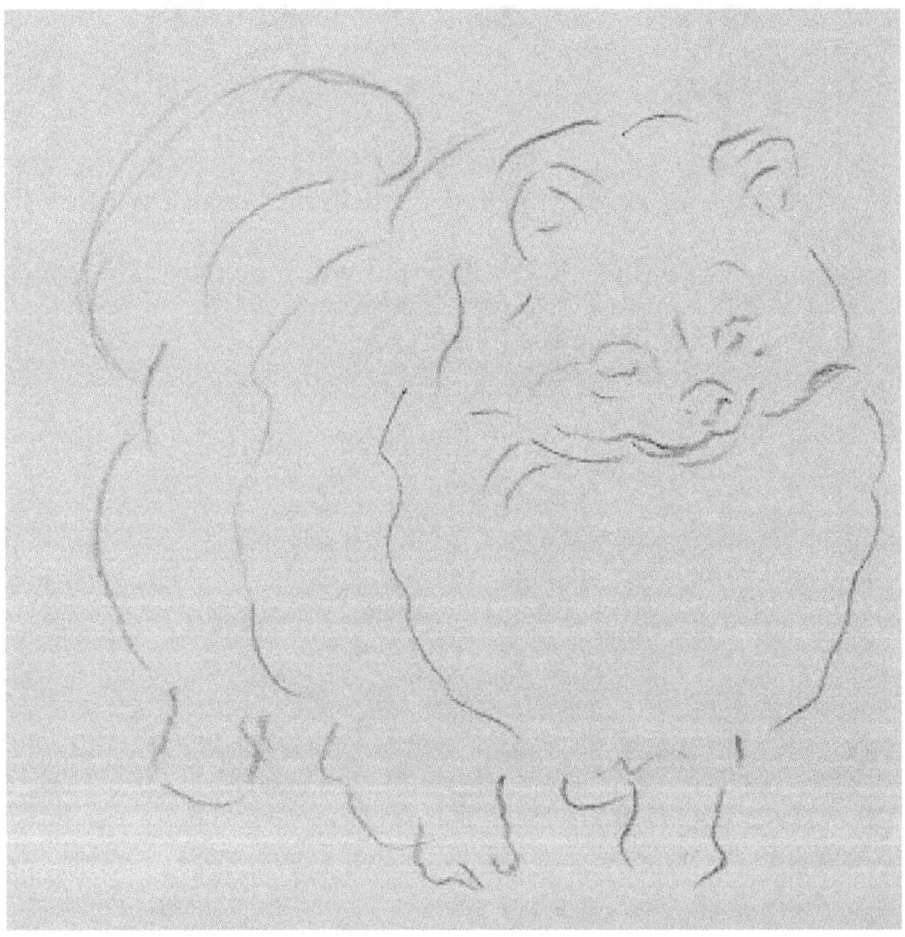

Draw the outline of the dog, using curved lines. Make the triangular ears and outline of the facial features

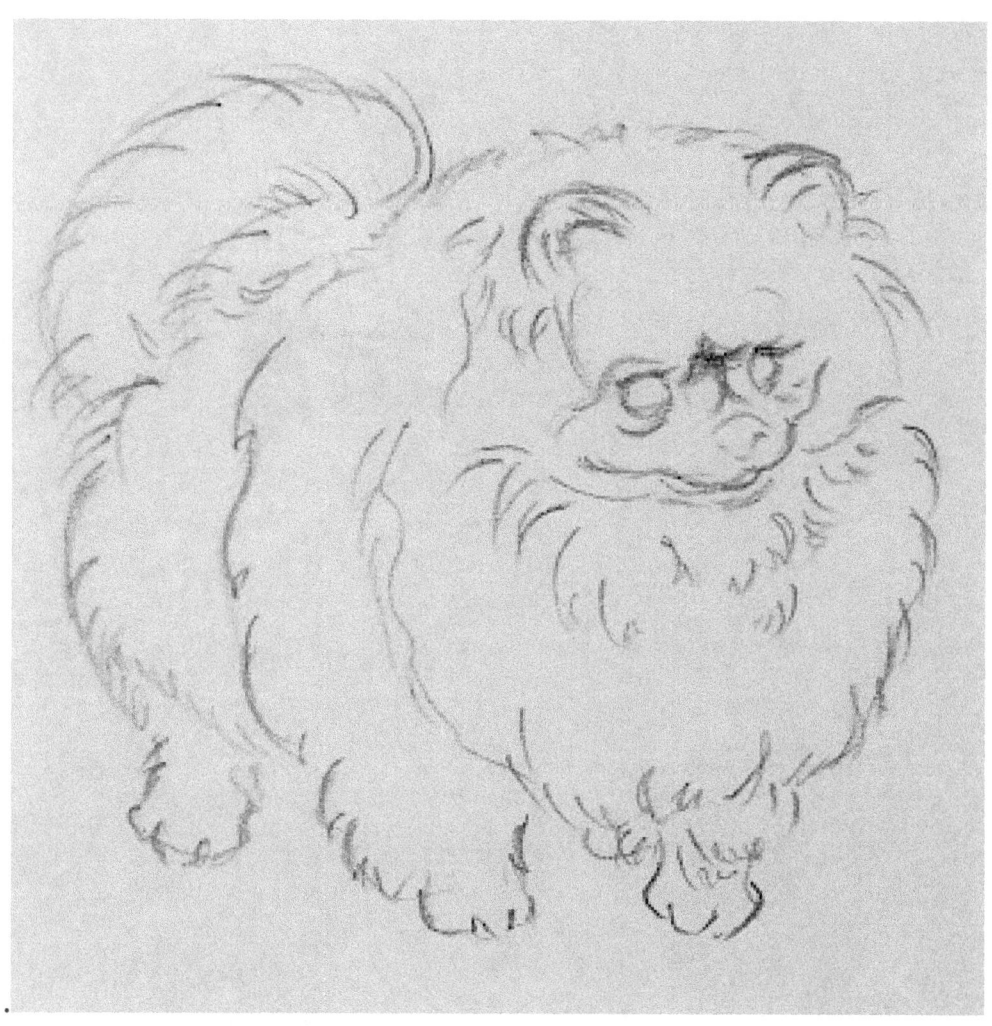

Go over the faint lines that you made with a series of pointed strokes to give

the illusion of fluffy fur. Go over the facial features with darker strokes.

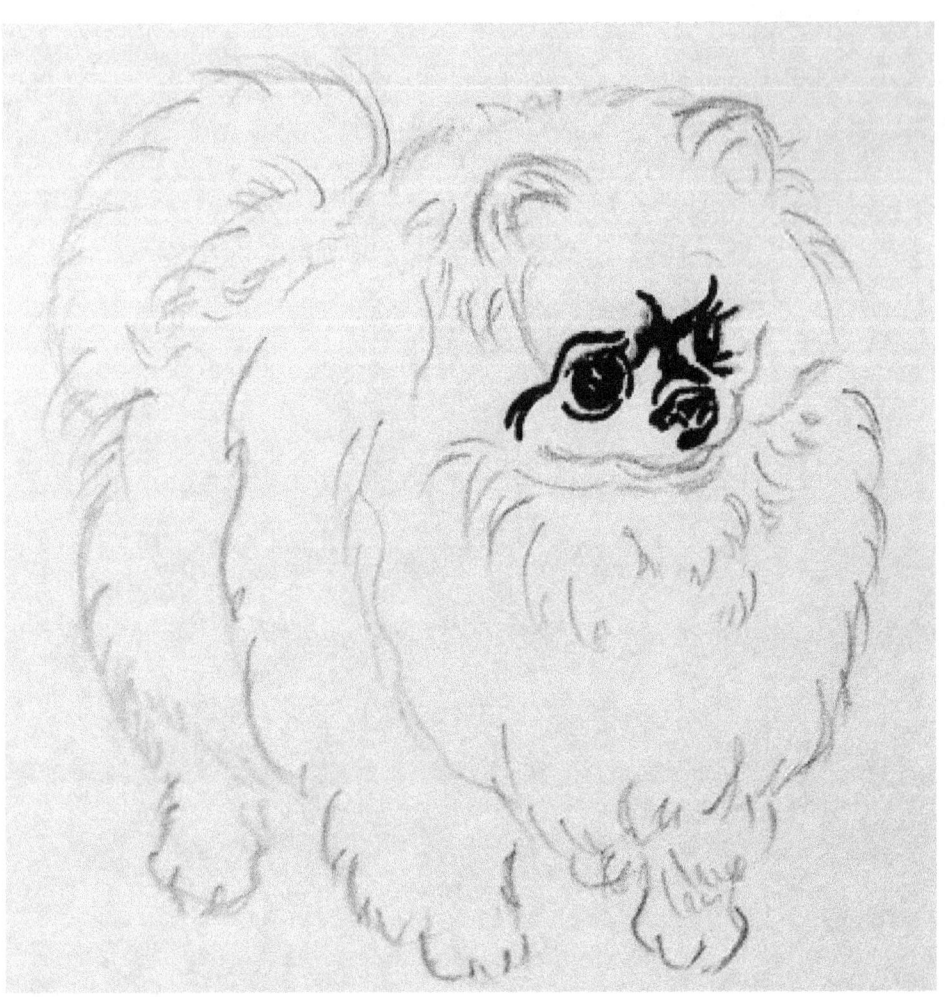

Go over the facial features (eyes and nose) with darker marks. Include dark

lines around the eyes and down the bridge of the nose.

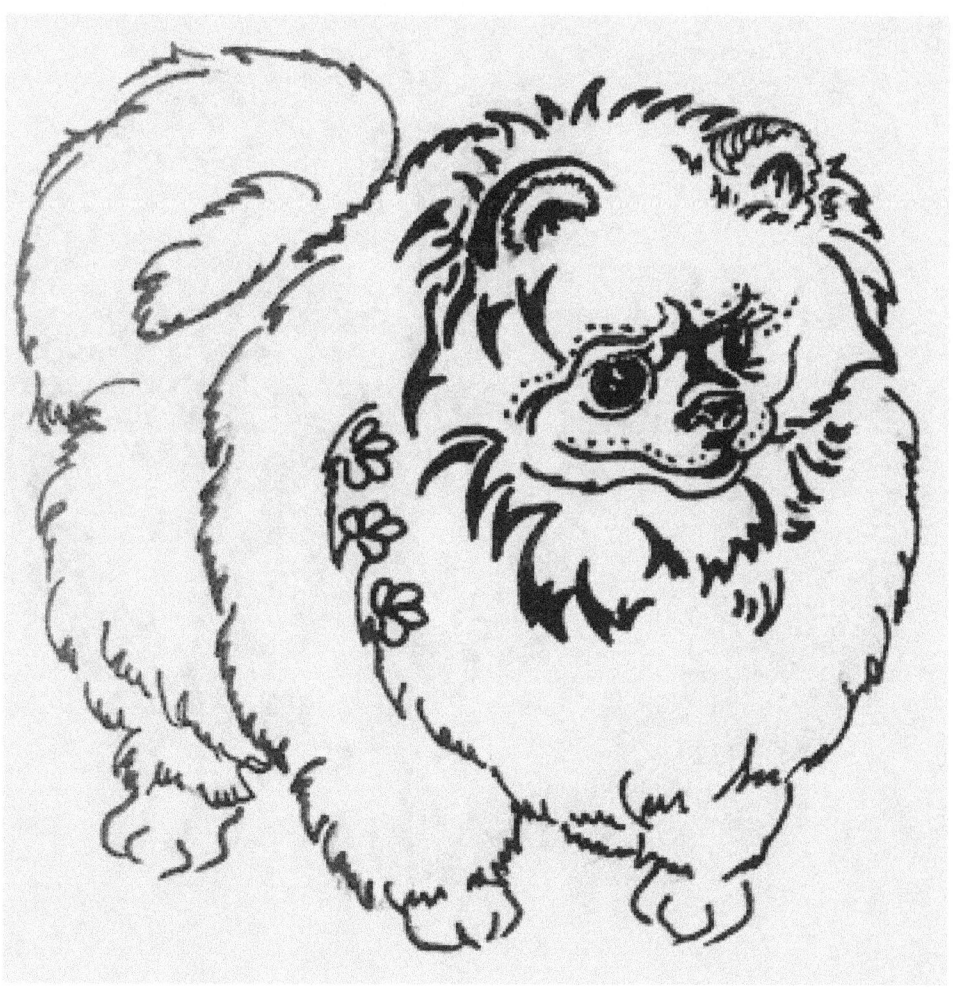

Go over the outline of the dog's fur with bold marks. On the animal's neck, include some thicker, bolder strokes for the fur. Draw in some small dots outlining the region above the eyes and along the upper portion of the mouth. Near the dog's right leg, make three floral patterns.

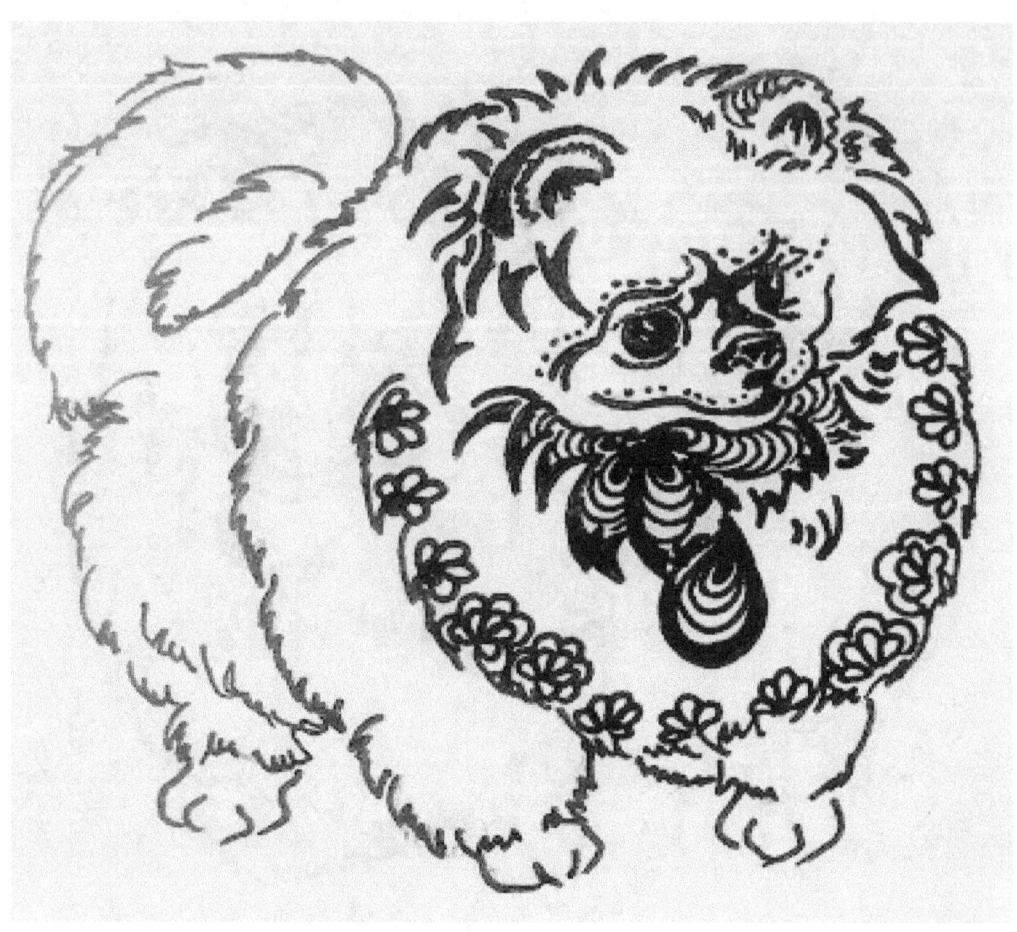

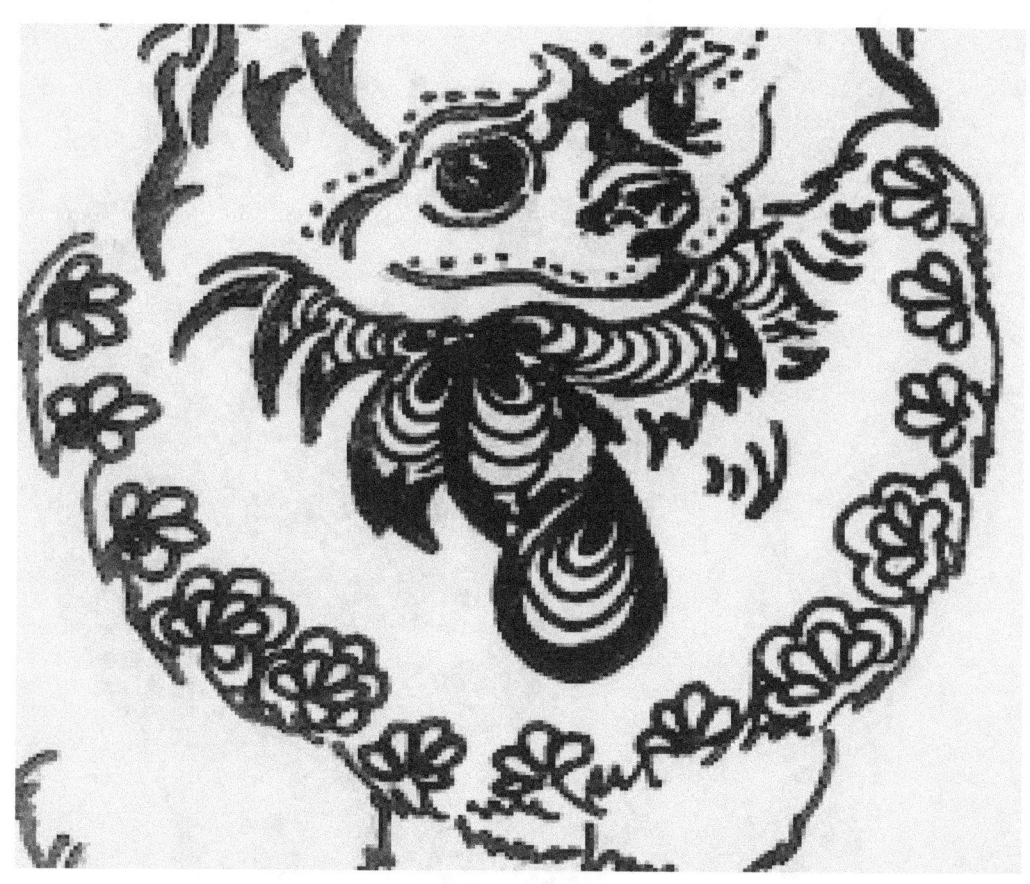

Continue with more floral patterns in a semi-circle above the front paws. Make some of the flowers larger along the bottom as indicated in the drawing. Beneath the mouth, make the triangular and tear drop patterns shown in the drawing. Draw the tips of the triangles and outline of the tear drops dark and bold. Inside of these shapes, make a series of concentric circles.

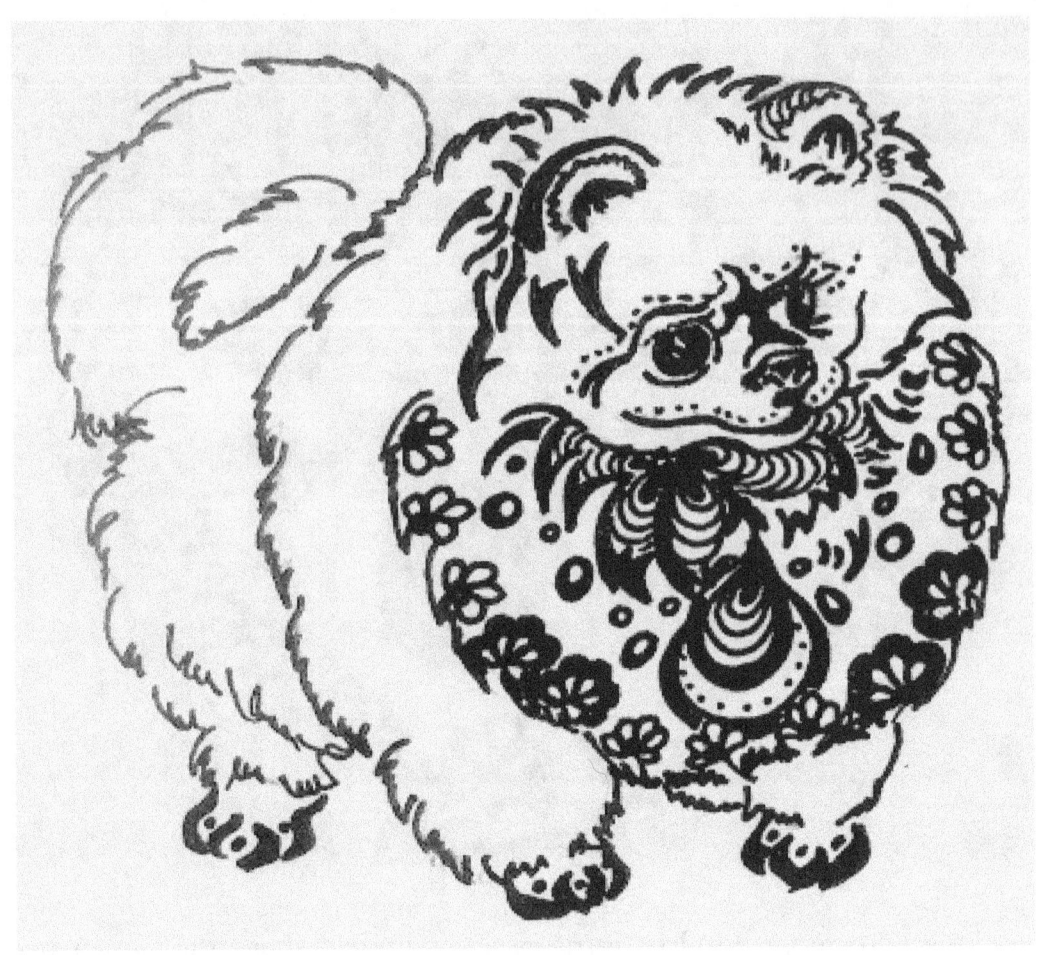

Go over the floral designs shown with bold shading. Put in several small circular shapes around the triangular and teardrop shapes. Fill in the round shapes, leaving a small portion of it unshaded. Put a semi-circular shape beneath the largest teardrop with dark shading on the outside of it and put a semi-circular line of dots inside of it. Go over the paws with thick, dark strokes and put a small dot on each toe.

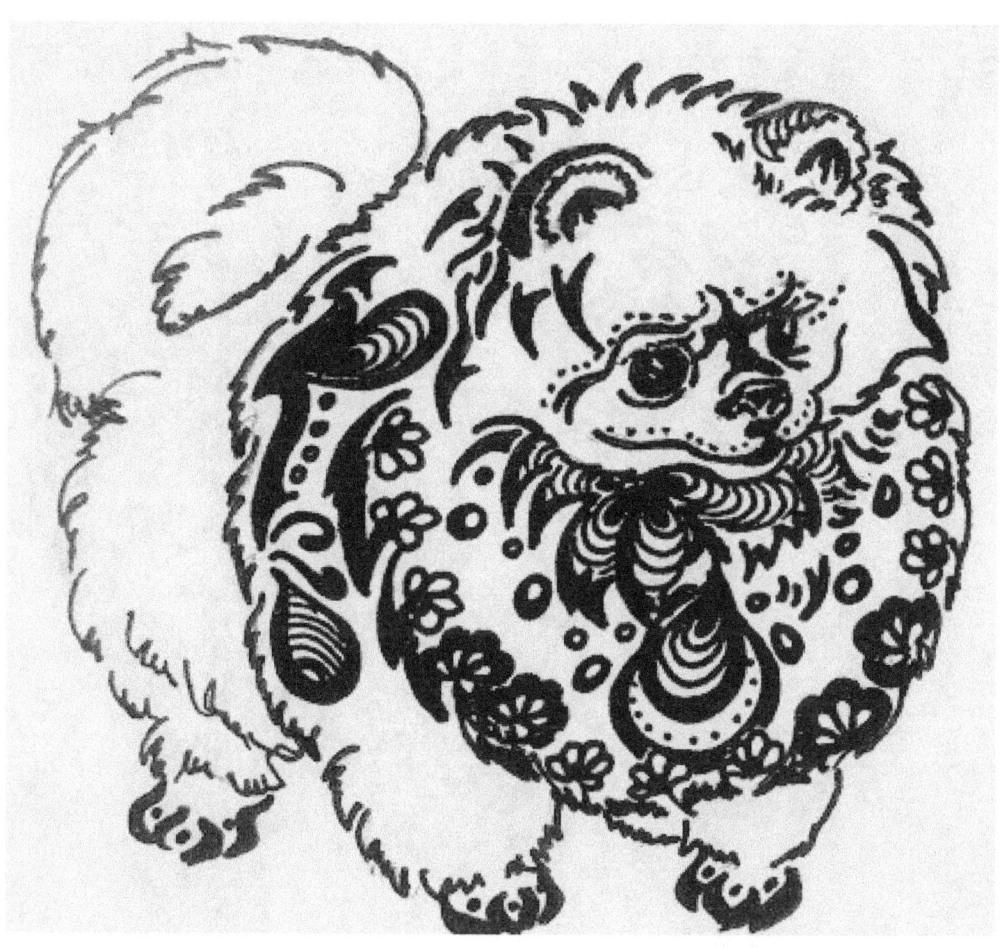

Above the dog's right, front paw, draw two more teardrop shapes and fill them with concentric circles. Make the outline of the shapes thick and bold. Draw in the thick, pointed lines connected to the upper teardrop and four small dots below it. Draw over the pointed lines connected to the floral patterns with thick, bold strokes.

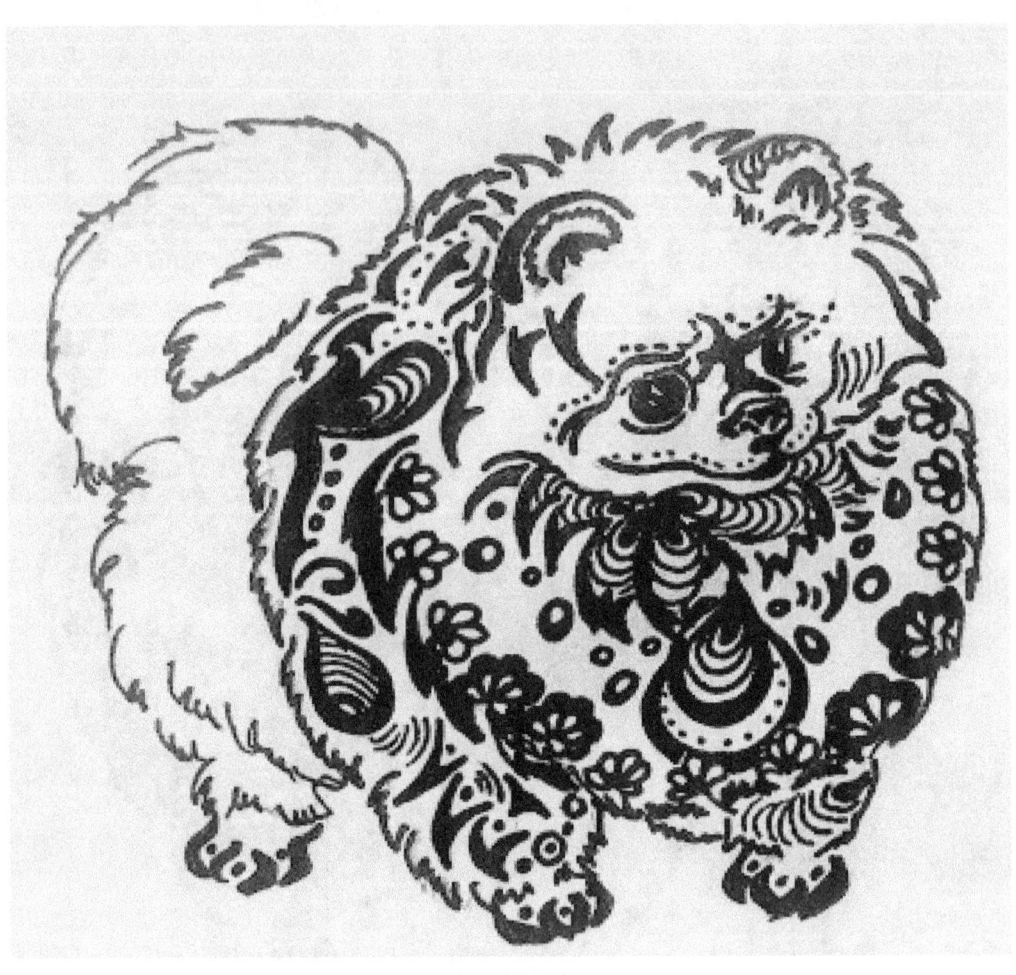

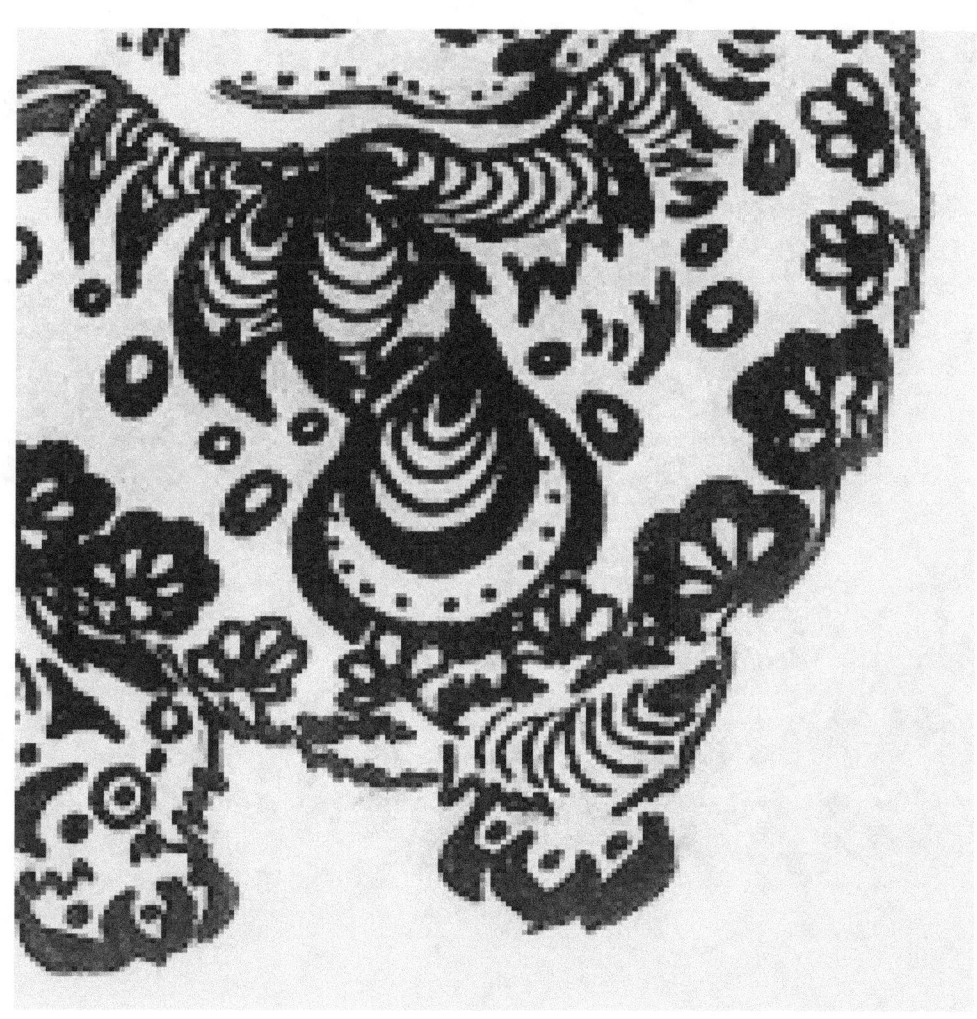

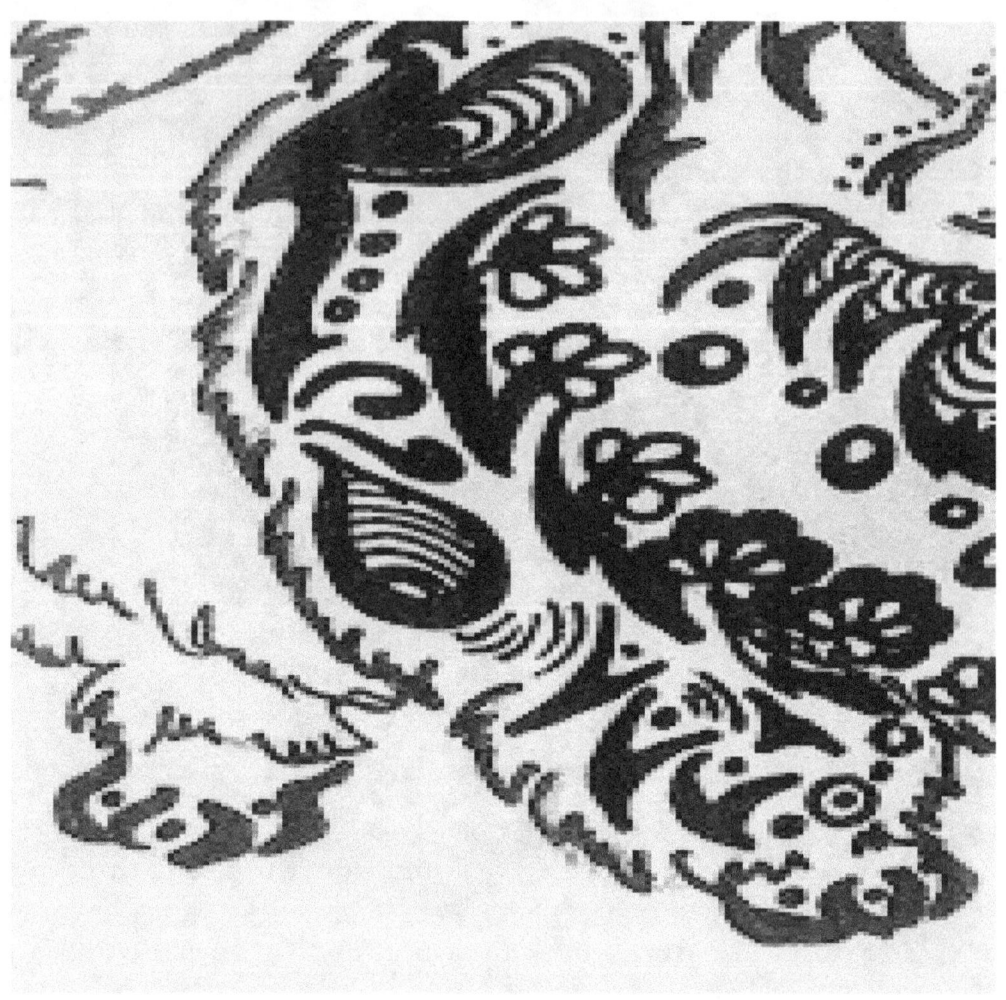

Draw in the triangular shapes shown in the drawing on the right, front leg and the various circles and concentric curved marks on both front legs and to the left of the dog's face.

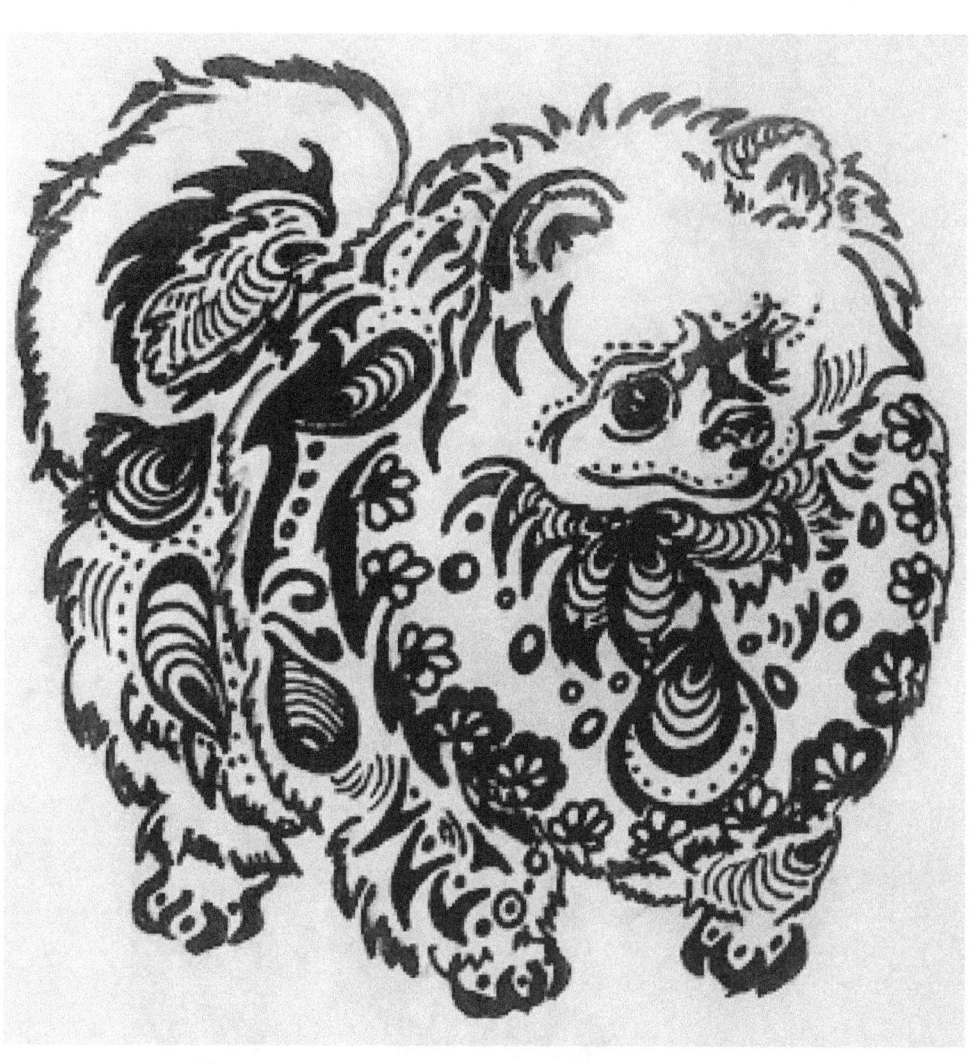

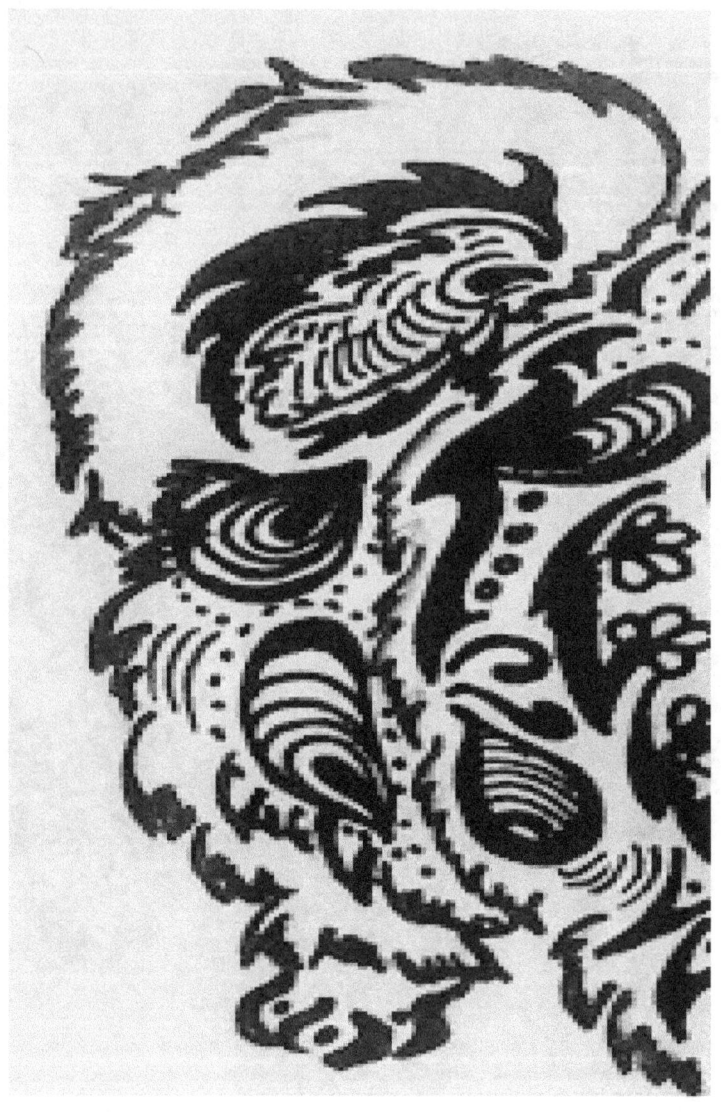

Draw in two more teardrop shapes on the rear leg and make concentric circles inside of them. Outline the shapes with the dotted lines and curved marks shown. On the underside of the tail, draw in the bold, pointed region shown in the drawing and the shape with concentric circles within it beneath this region.

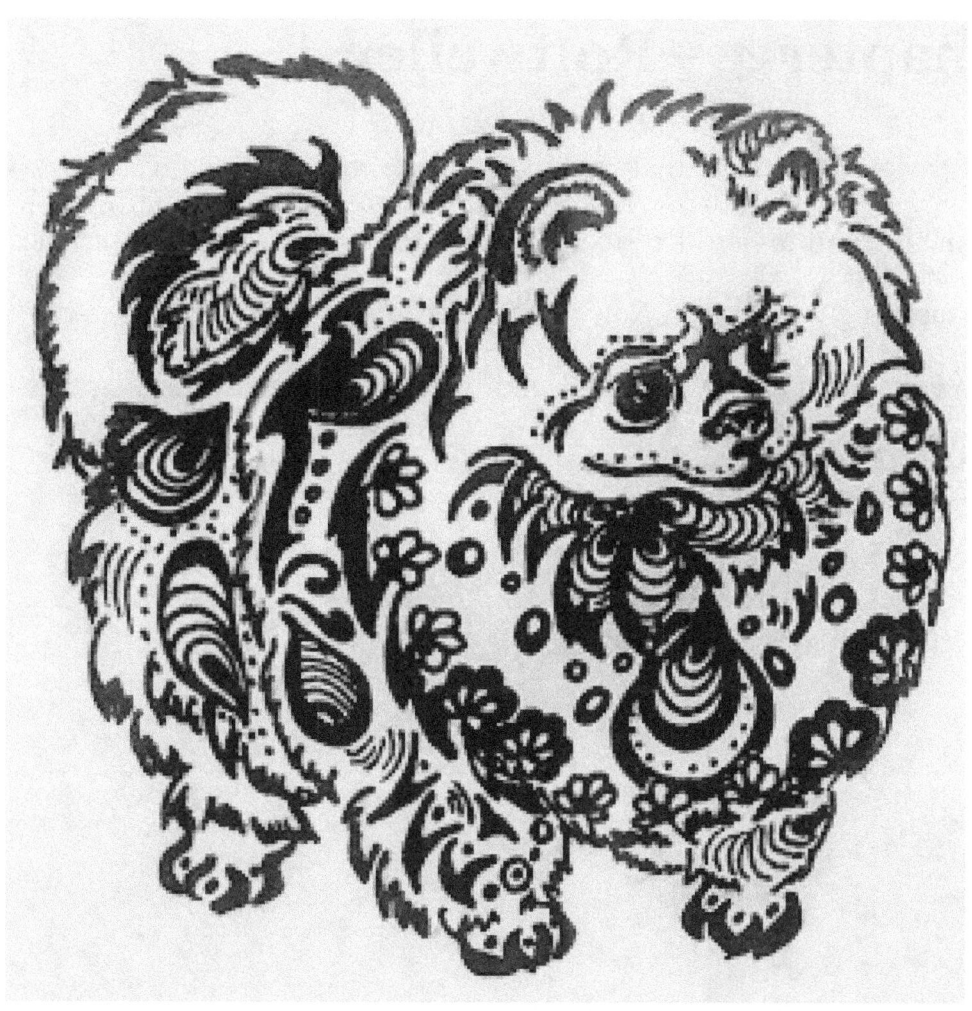

Here is a look at the completed drawing. Now is your chance to look over it to see if you have left out any of the details.

Chapter 4 – Rottweiler

Rottweilers are dogs that originally come from Germany. They were originally used to herd livestock; but also to pull carts carrying products to the market such as meat. Now, they are still used for herding livestock; but also as guide dogs for the blind and handicapped, guard dogs and search and rescue dogs!

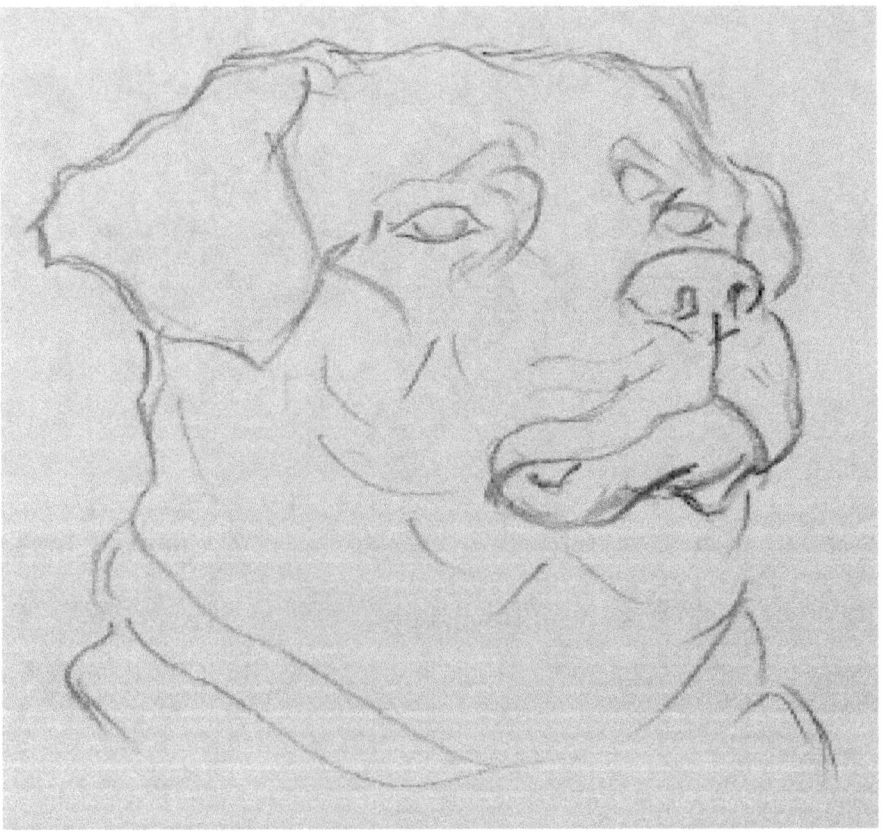

Sketch the dog's head, giving it a thick neck and short, floppy ears. Make its jowls slightly droopy and draw in the eyes and nose. Be sure to include the small marks on its face, mouth, and neck

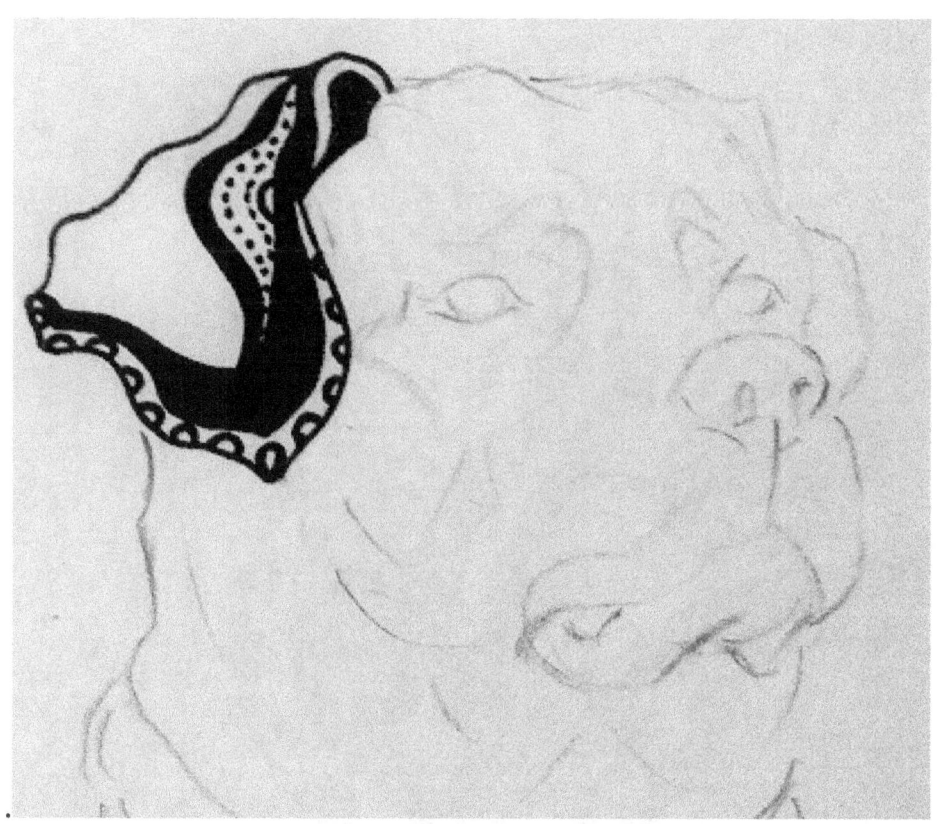

Go over the ear with bold, dark marks. On the lower edge of the ear, make a series of dark semi-circles. Above this, shade in a thick region of black. Make a curved stripe with dotted lines within it on the upper portion of the ear. Leave a curved stripe at the top of the ear with no shading.

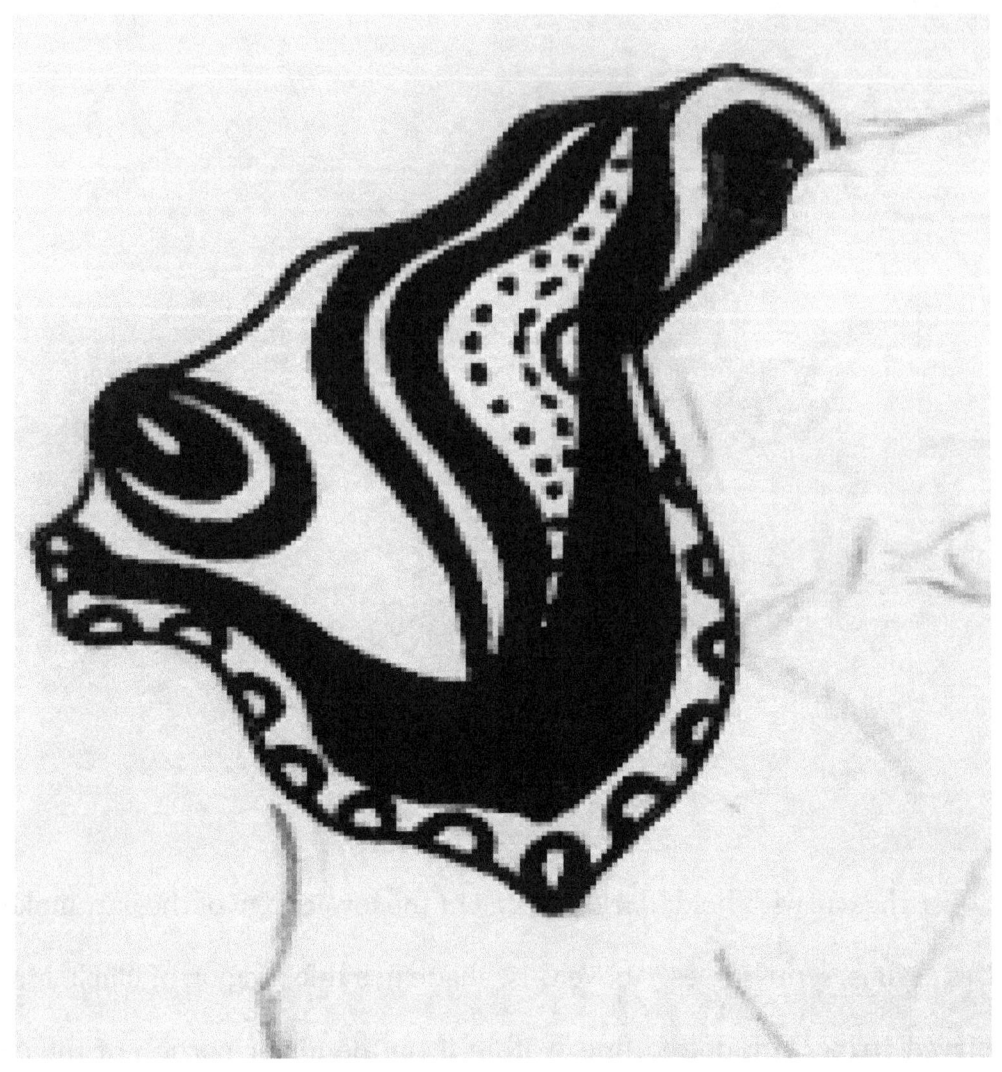

On the left side of the ear, make an oval shape. Leave a moon-shaped portion of the ear unshaded, along with a tiny dot above it.

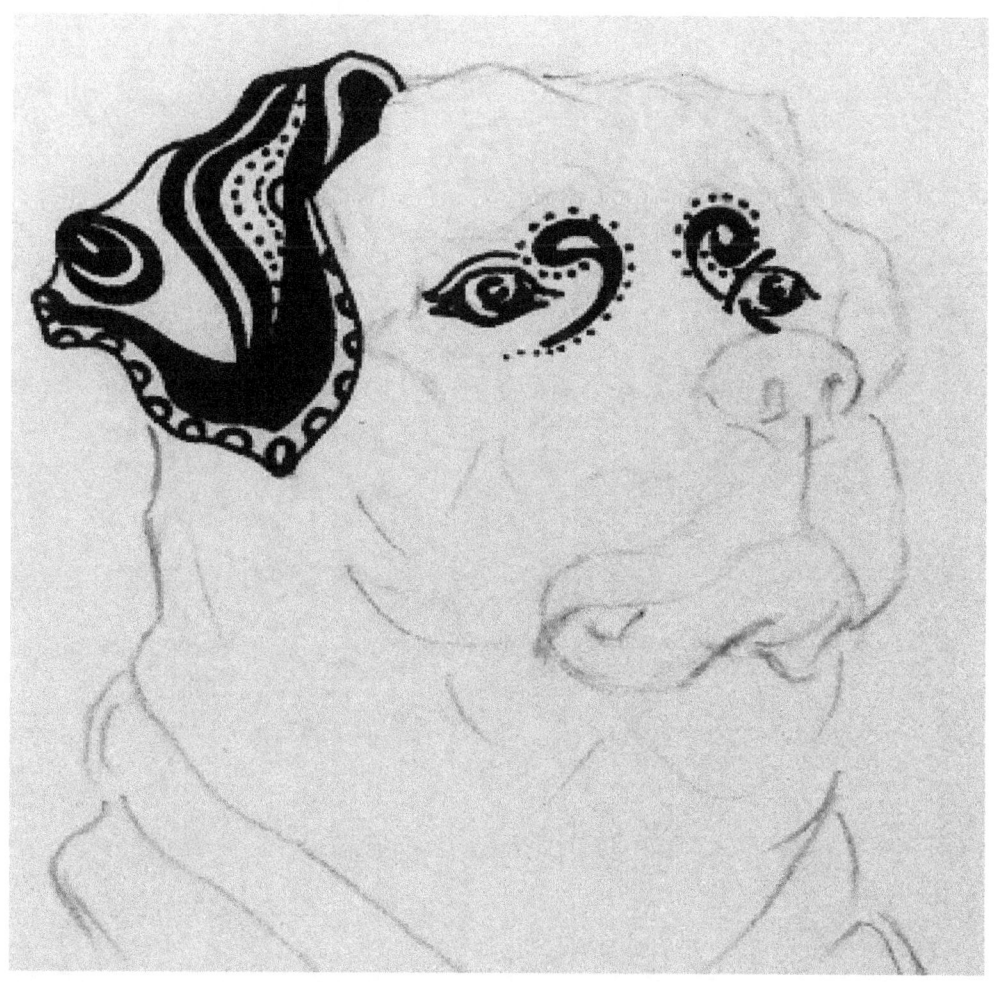

Go over the eyes with bold marks leaving small 'C' shapes inside the eye. Make two bold, thick curved shapes extending from the bridge of the nose, between the eyes. Along the curved shapes, make a line of dots around each one.

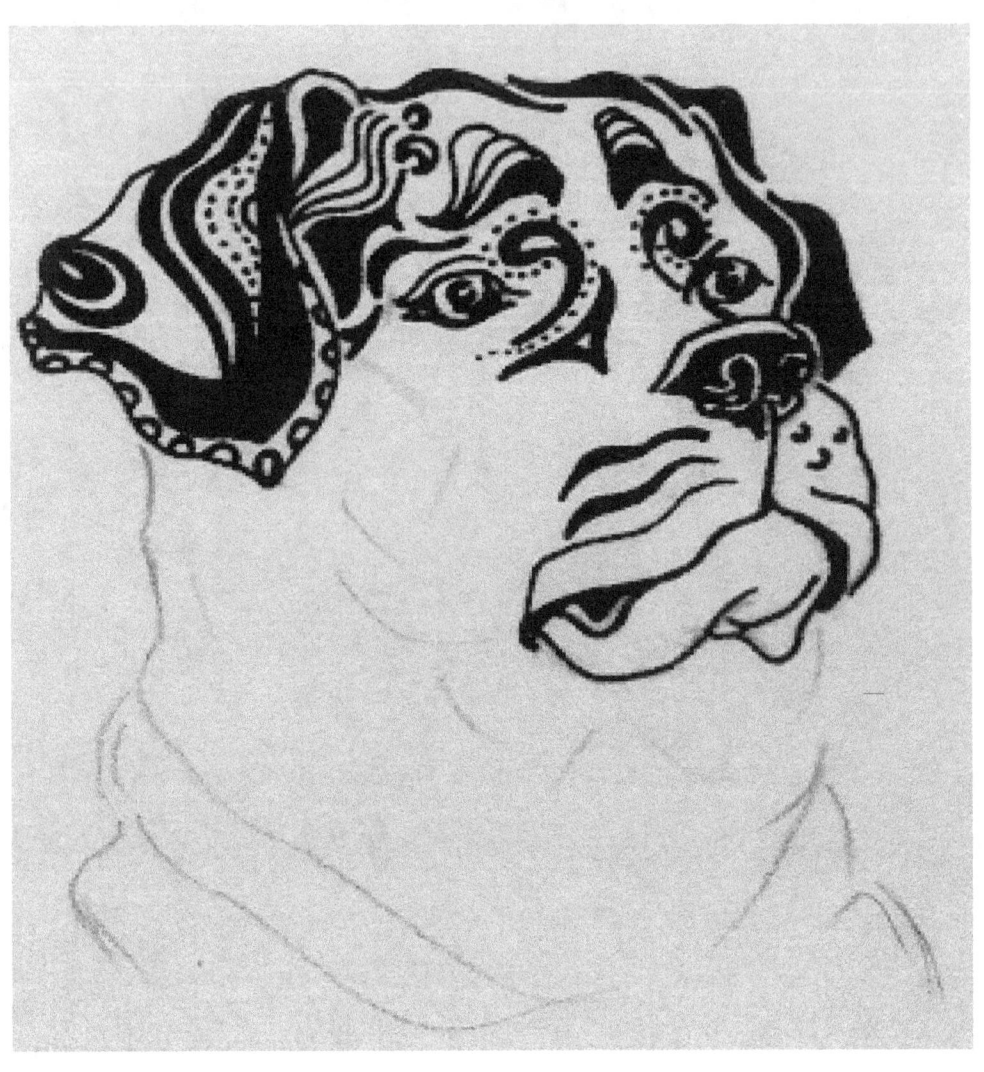

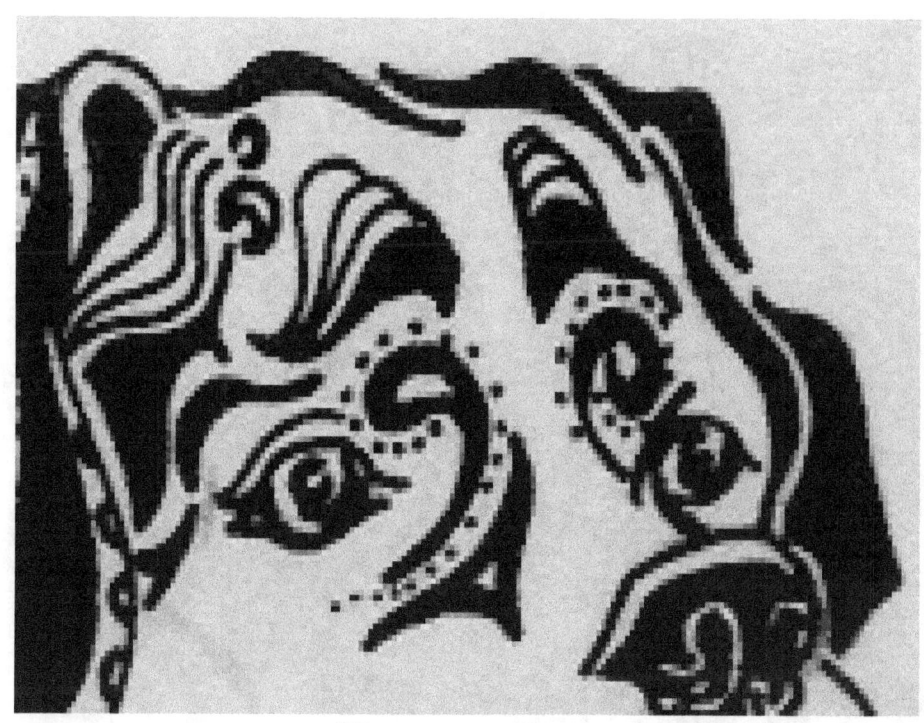

Above the eyes, make two irregular, curved shapes with the bottom shapes shaded in. Just to the right of the ear, make the irregular shaded regions and concentric curved lines above these. Draw in the triangular shape beneath the right eye. Go over the nose and mouth with bold marks as indicated in the drawing. Shade in the small portion of the left ear boldly.

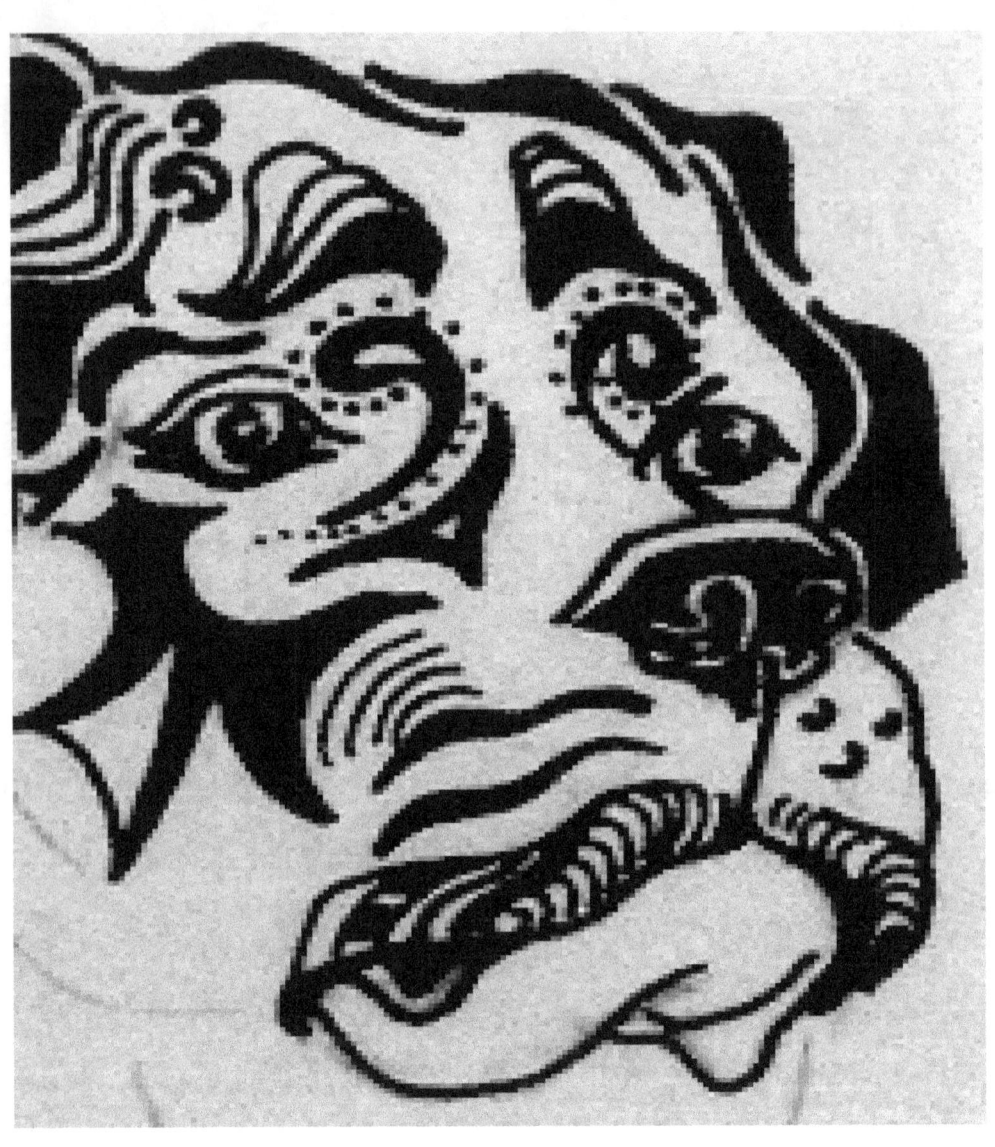

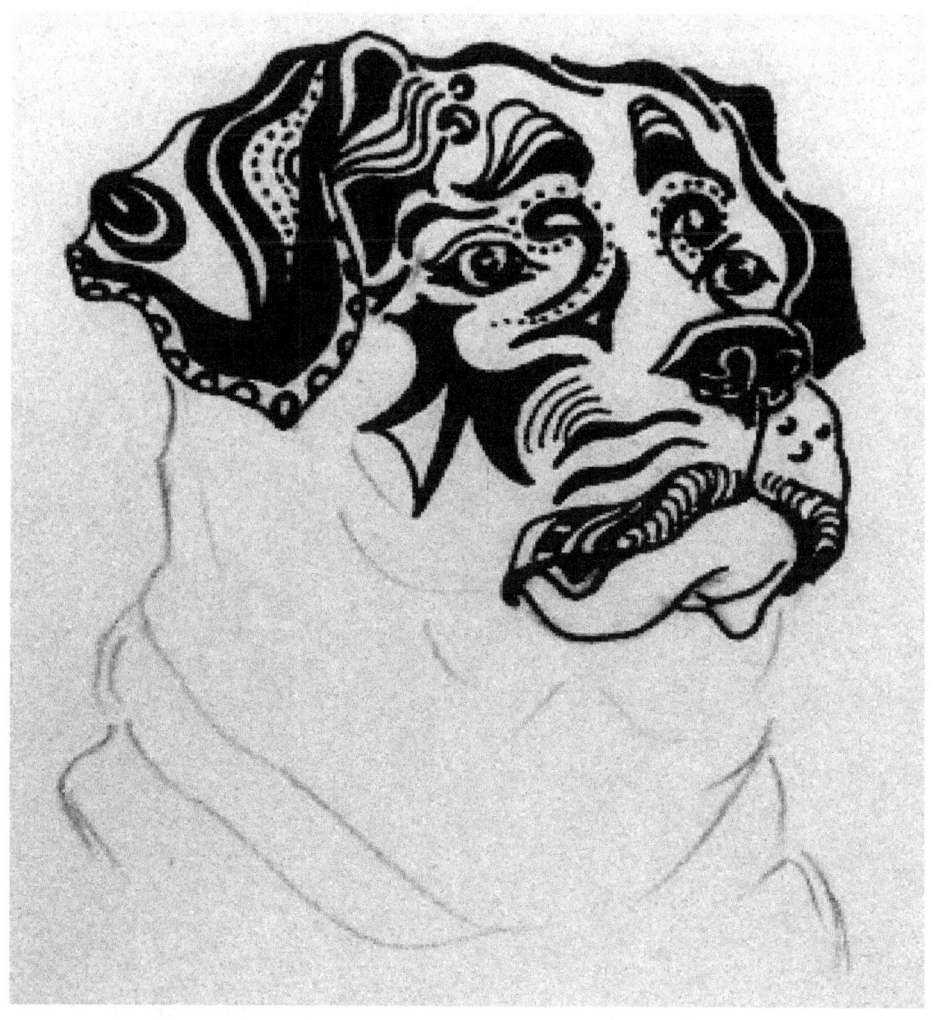

Make the thick, bat-like shape on the lower right portion of the dog's face, leaving a small triangular shape unshaded. Along the upper portion of the mouth, make the alternating bands of dotted lines, unshaded lines, shaded lines and concentric curved marks.

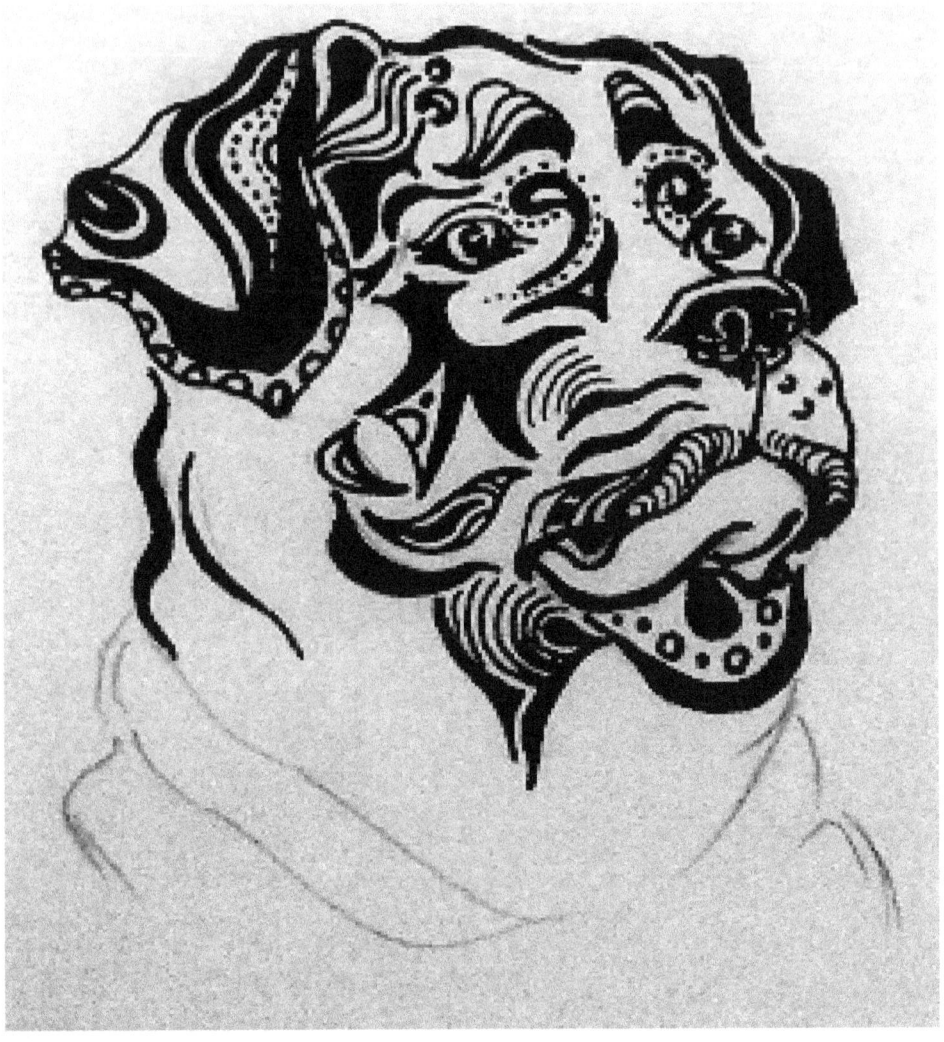

Beneath the dog's jowls, make a semi-circular shape that has a thick, bold outline. Put in the circular shapes inside of it and a shaded, pear shape above the circles. On the lower, right portion of the face, make the irregular, curved shapes shown in the drawing. Be sure to include the bold, shaded regions and concentric curved marks shown in the drawing.

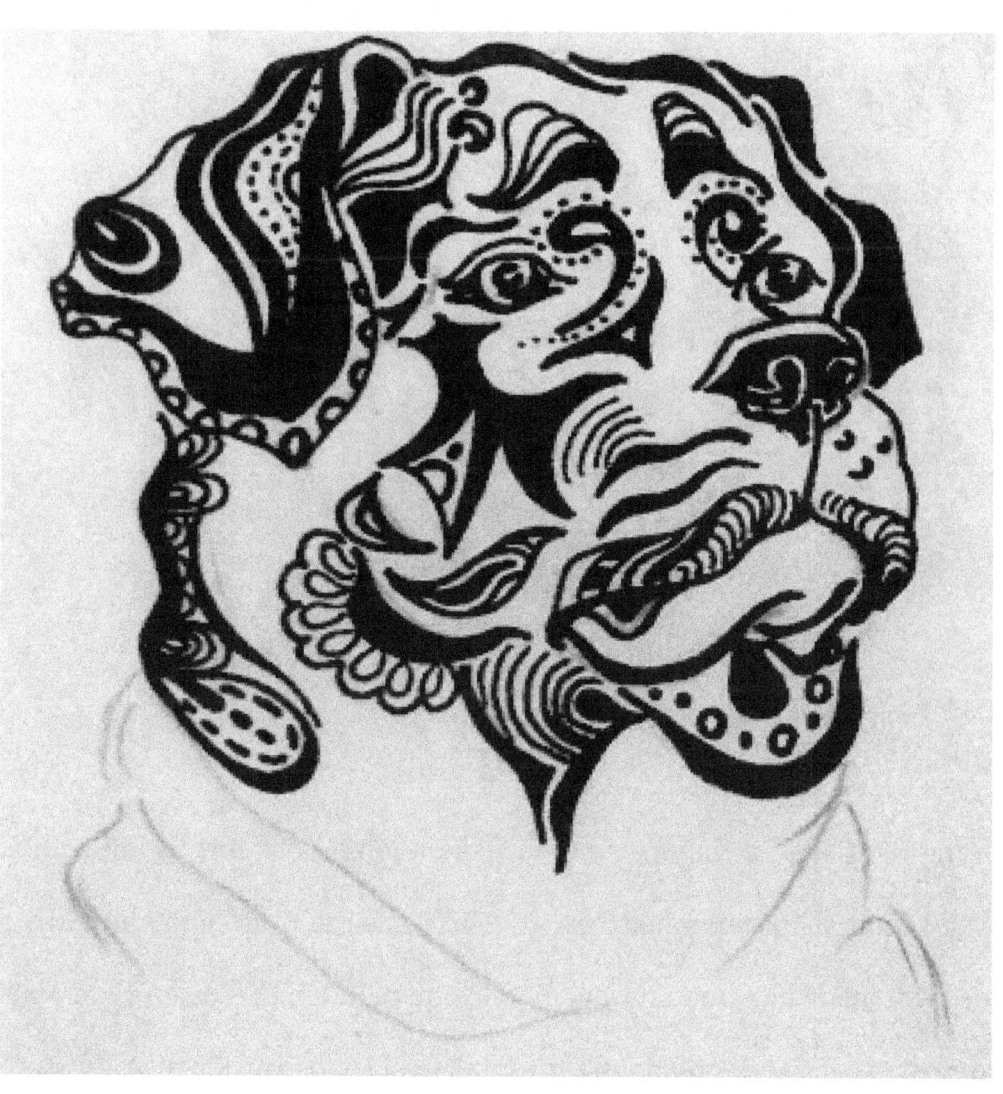

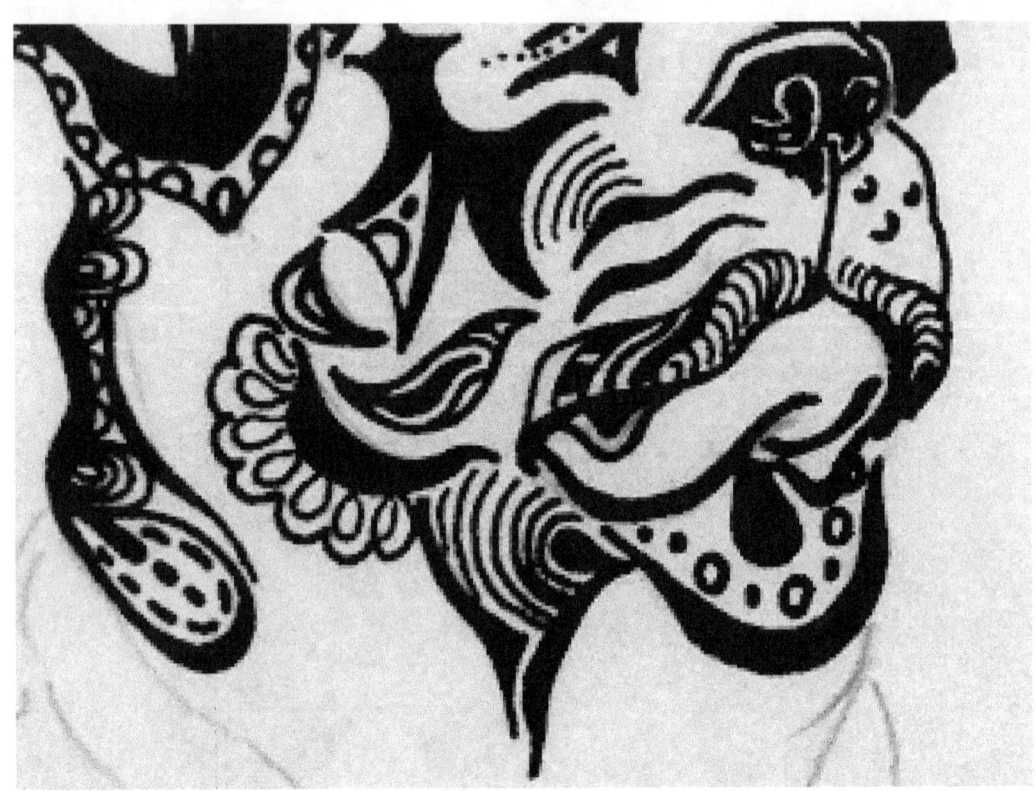

On the right side of the dog's neck, make a long, bold curved line and add several loop shapes coming from it. Make a large oval shape beneath the loops you made and put a dashed line inside of it. On the lower, right side of the face, make a series of loops with small oval shapes inside of it.

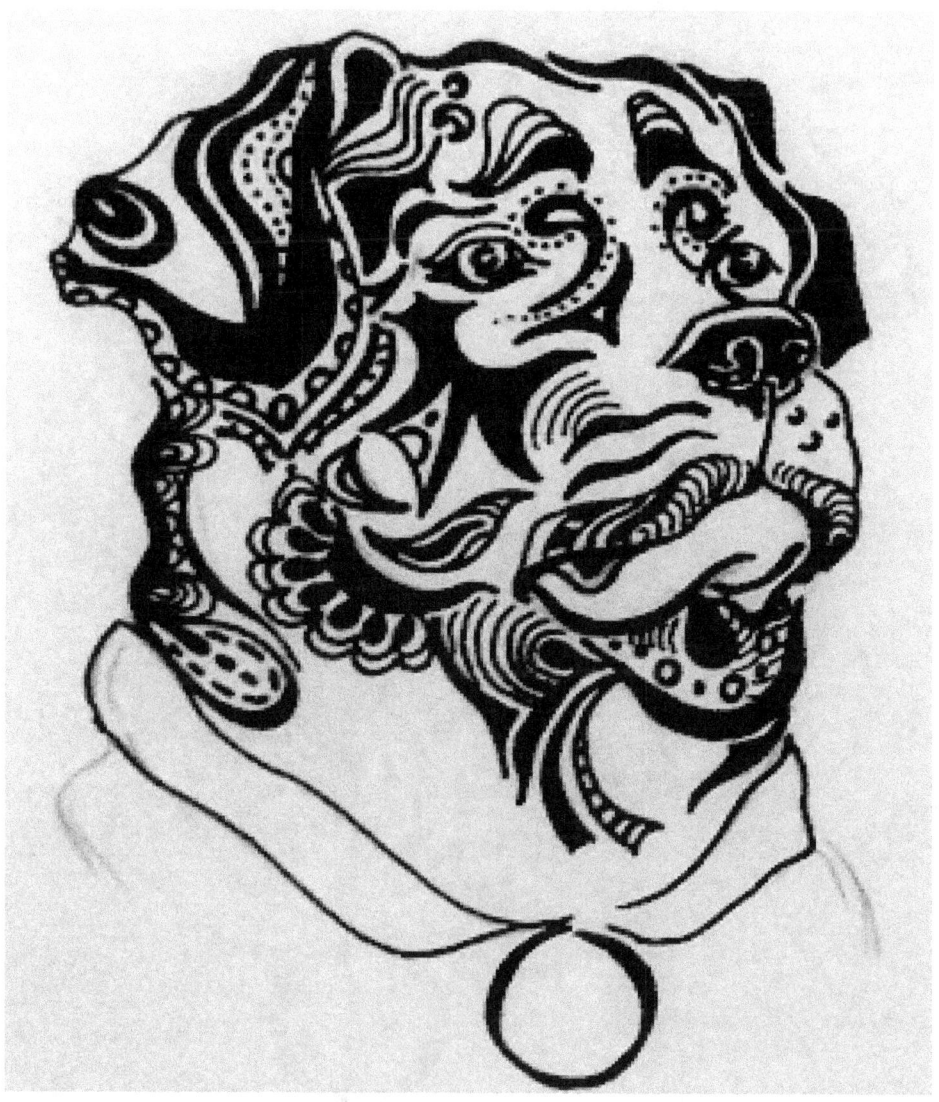

Outline the folds of the neck with bold marks. Make a round shape in the middle that will be the dog's tag. Draw I the small, irregular bold shape on the left side of the neck and the ladder-like shape on the right.

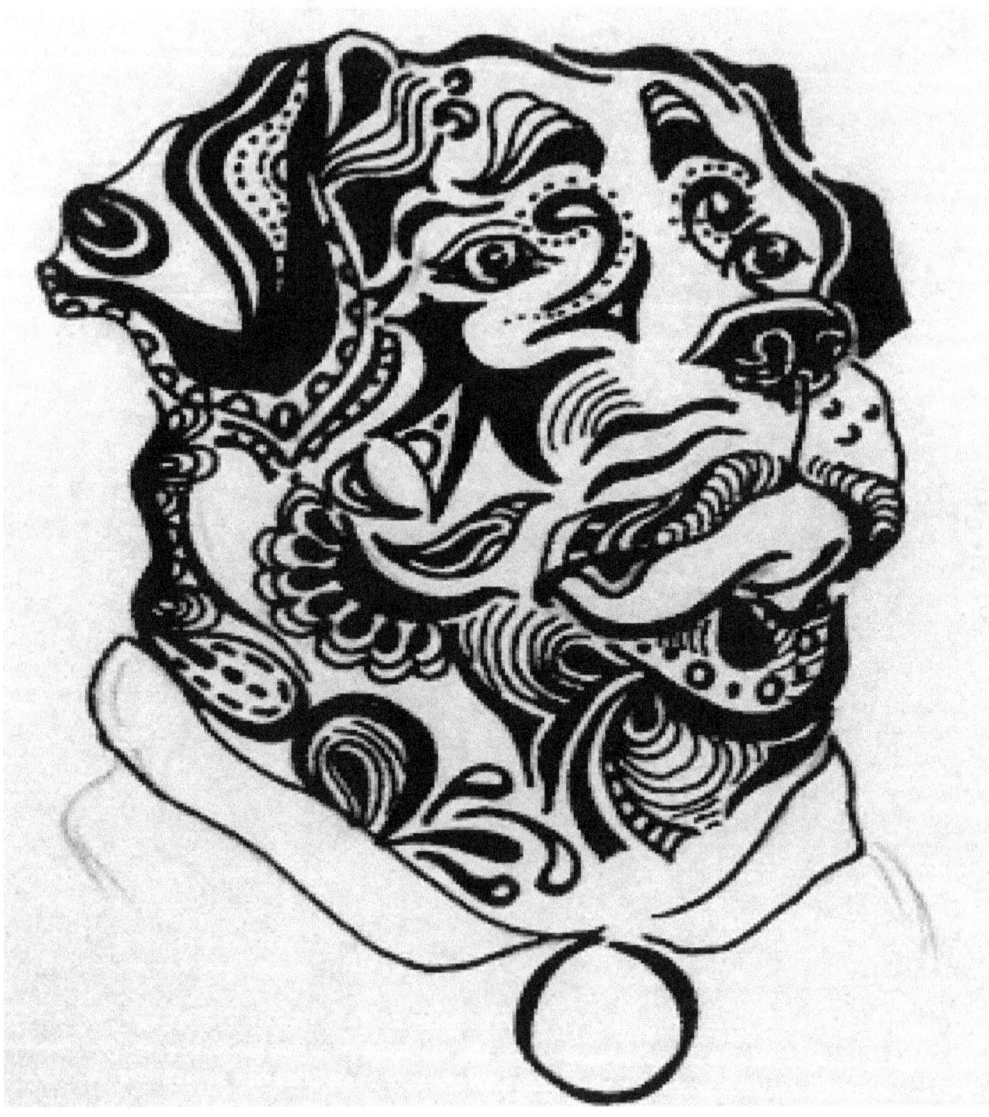

Make concentric circles between the shaded shape and ladder-like shape you just made. Make the large tear drop shape and four smaller teardrop shapes on the lower right portion of the neck. Be sure to include the shaded regions and concentric lines within the large teardrop.

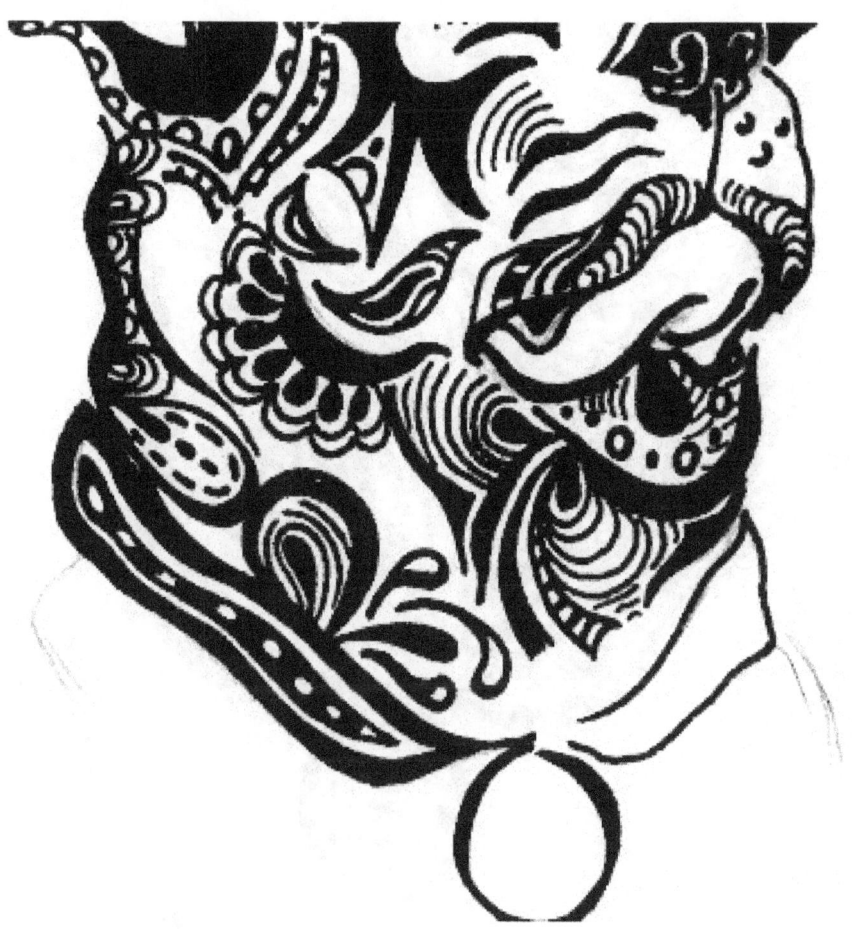

Make a long, bean-like shape as part of the dog's collar. Outline the edges boldly, leaving an area unshaded underneath this. Inside the bean-like shape, make another bean-like shape with eight small ovals inside of it. Shade in the inner bean-shape but do not shade the small ovals.

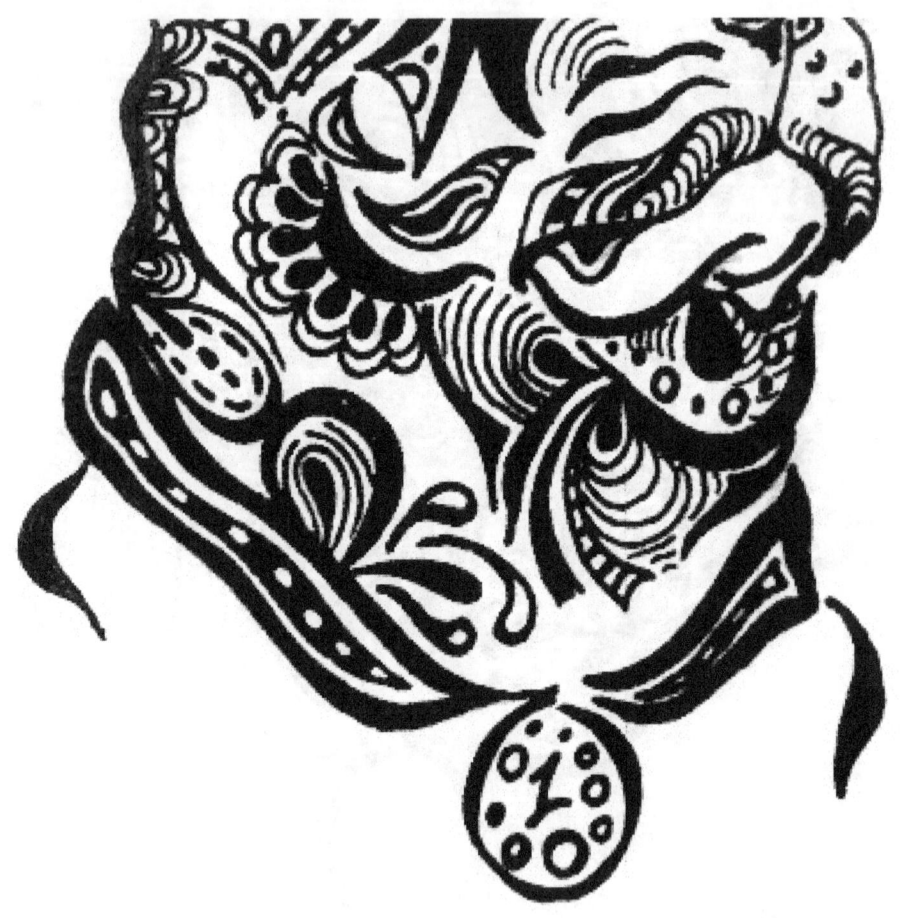

Within the dog's tag, make a series of circular shapes and draw a large number '1' in the center. On the left side of the collar, make a very bold line with a region inside of it that will be unshaded. Inside the unshaded portion, make a rectangular shape that is shaded with a few circles inside of it that should be left unshaded. Make two shaded, curved shapes extending from each side of the collar.

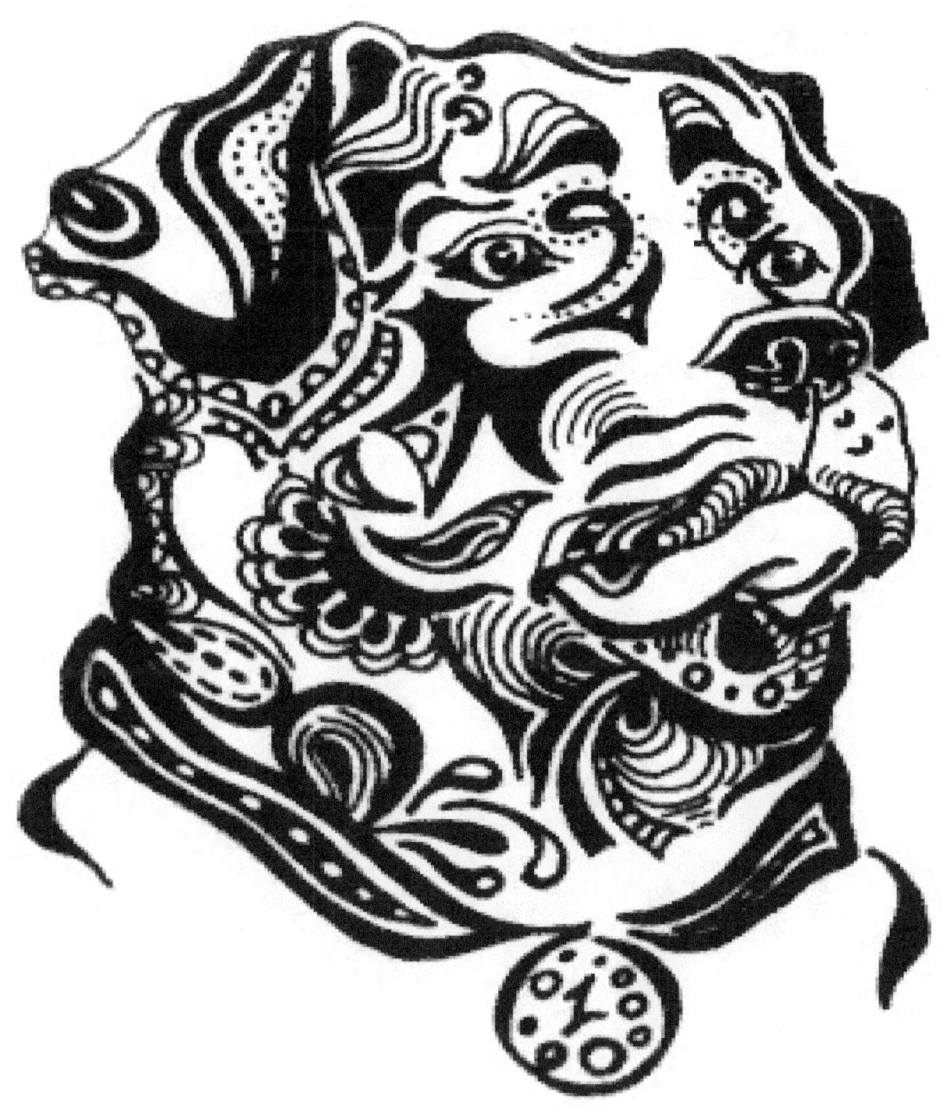

Here is a look at the completed drawing. Now, look over the detail and make
sure that you haven't left anything out.

Chapter 5 – Corgi

Corgis were originally from Wales where they were used as herding dogs. They are known for their long bodies, long ears, and short, stubby legs. These dogs are very active and vocal; and they need exercise on a regular basis. They are playful and devoted; but also bold and protective.

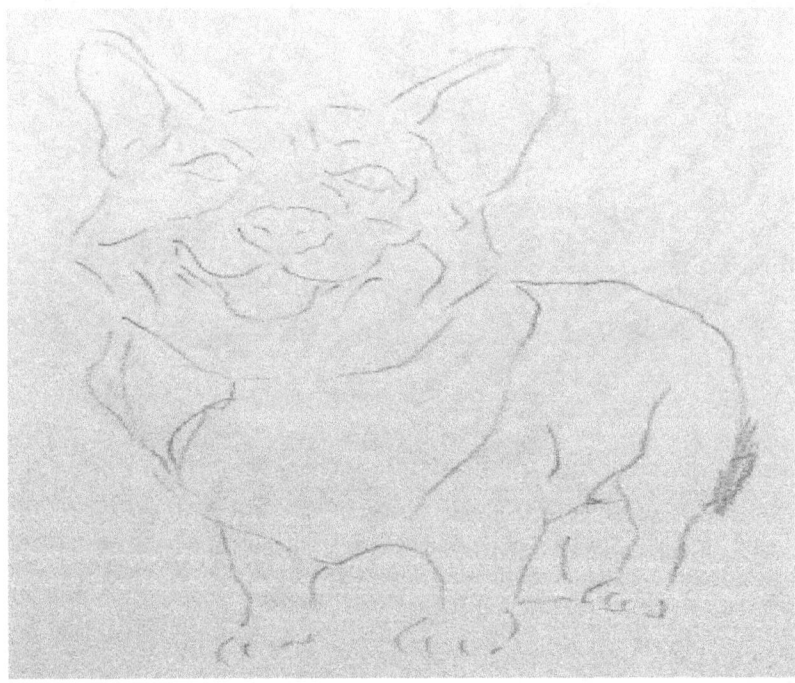

Make the sketch of the dog's long, pointed ears, short stocky body and legs. For the face, make two oval-shaped eyes, a roundish nose, and a tongue extended out. Be sure to include the lines on its face, around its mouth and along its neck and chest.

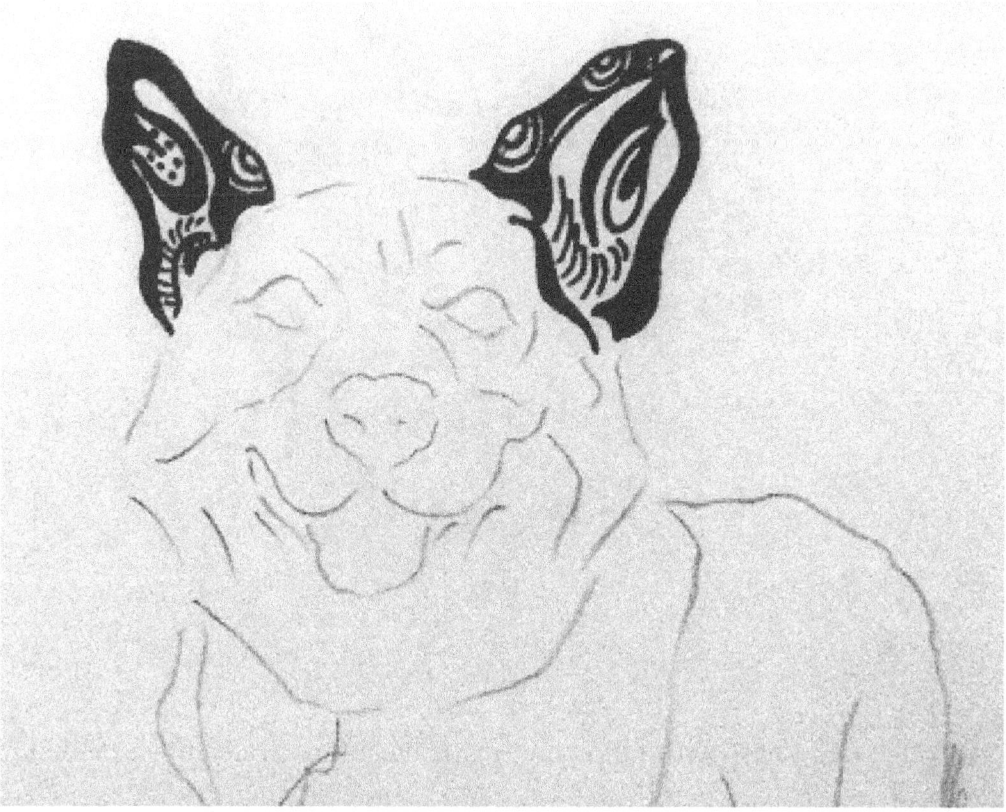

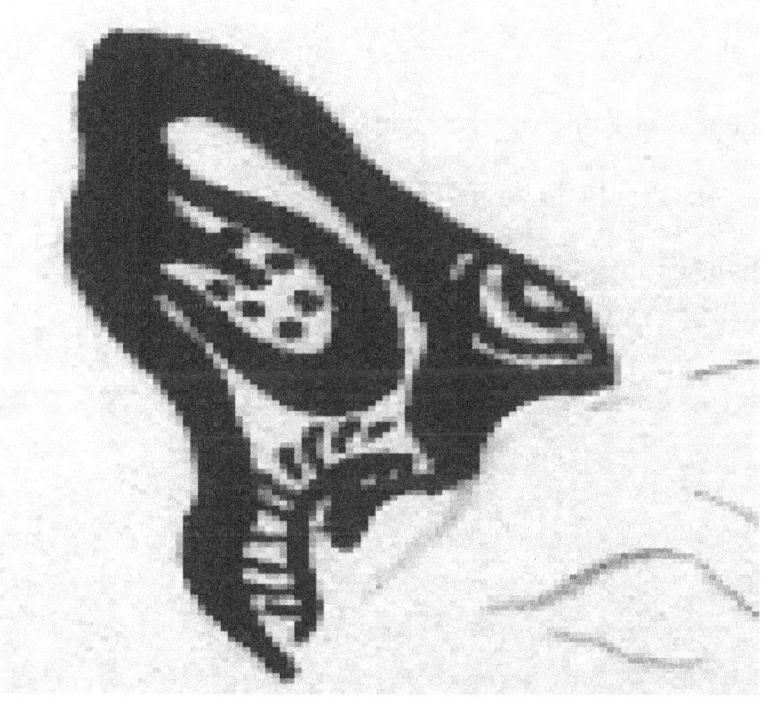

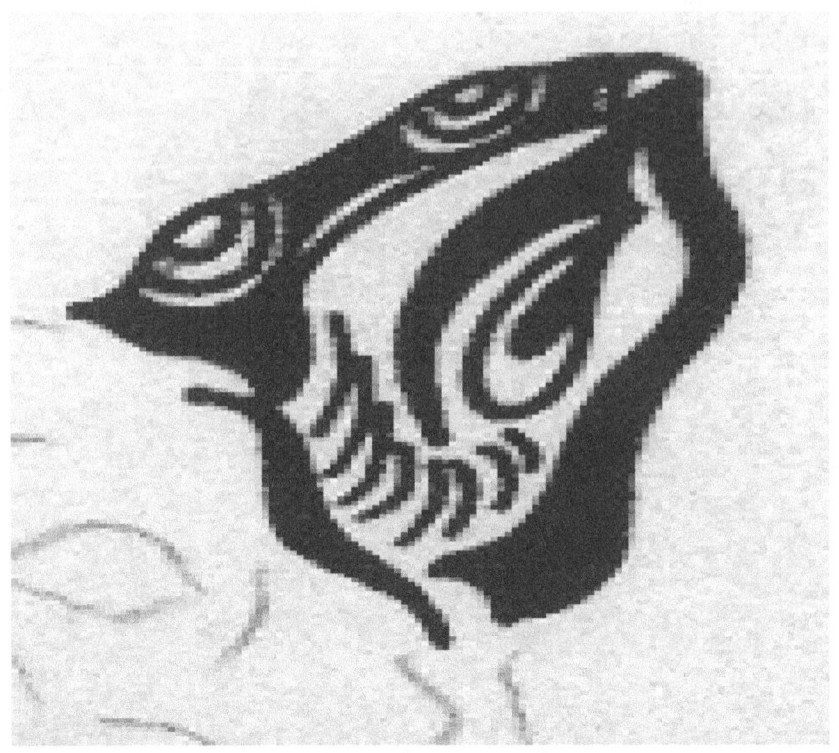

Outline the dog's ears with bold shading, leave a few circles unshaded along the edge. In these unshaded regions, make concentric circles. Inside the ears, along the bottom, make a series of curved marks. Inside the ear make two oval shapes. The one on the right should include dots inside of it. The one on the left should have a shaded area inside of it and a large, bold irregular shape connected to it.

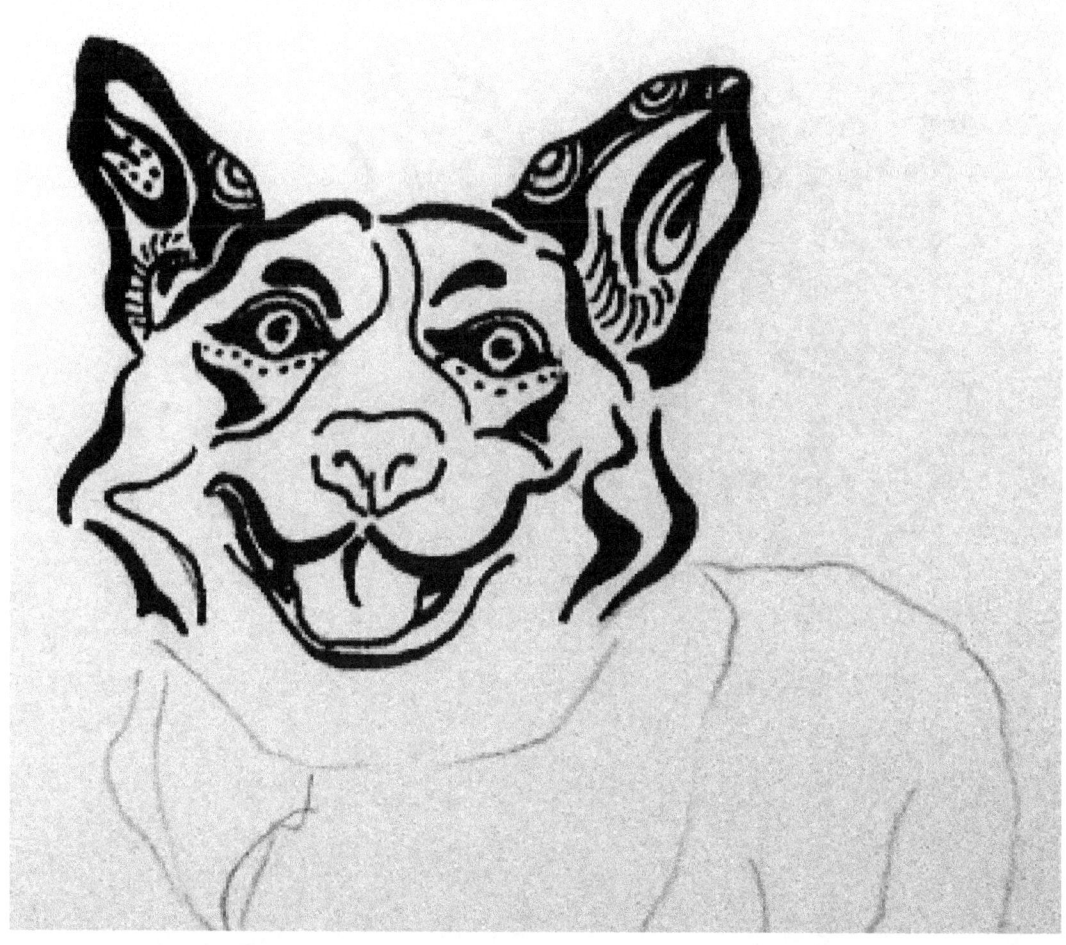

Go over the outline of the dog's head with bold, mustache-like marks. Draw lines that curve outwards down the bridge of the nose. Give the dog bold, teardrop shaped eyebrows and darken in the eyes, leaving an unshaded region and small, shaded, 'c' shapes inside the unshaded region. Go over the nose and mouth with bold marks.

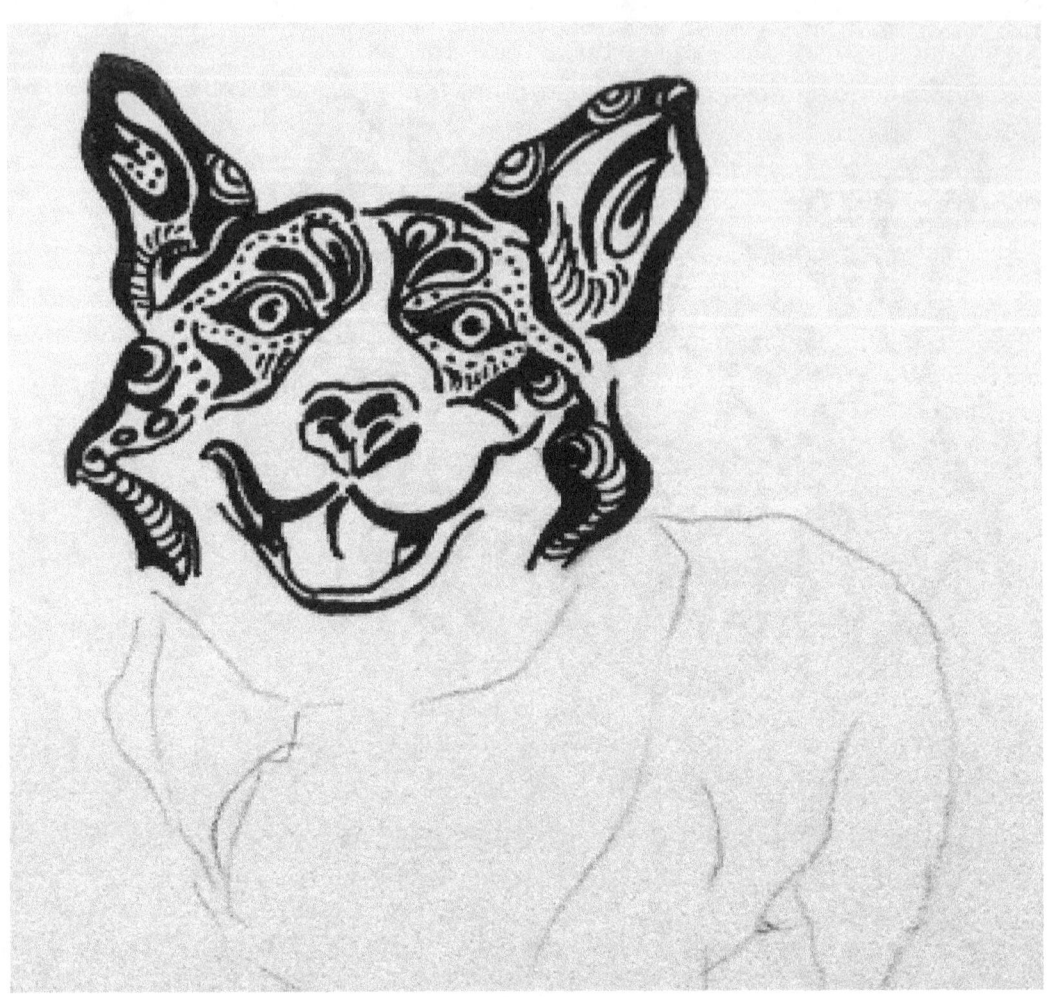

Make a series of dotted lines around the eyes as shown in the drawing. Add some small circles and concentric curved lines along lower sides of the head. Add a couple of small teardrop shapes above each eye. Add some bold marks on the dog's nose.

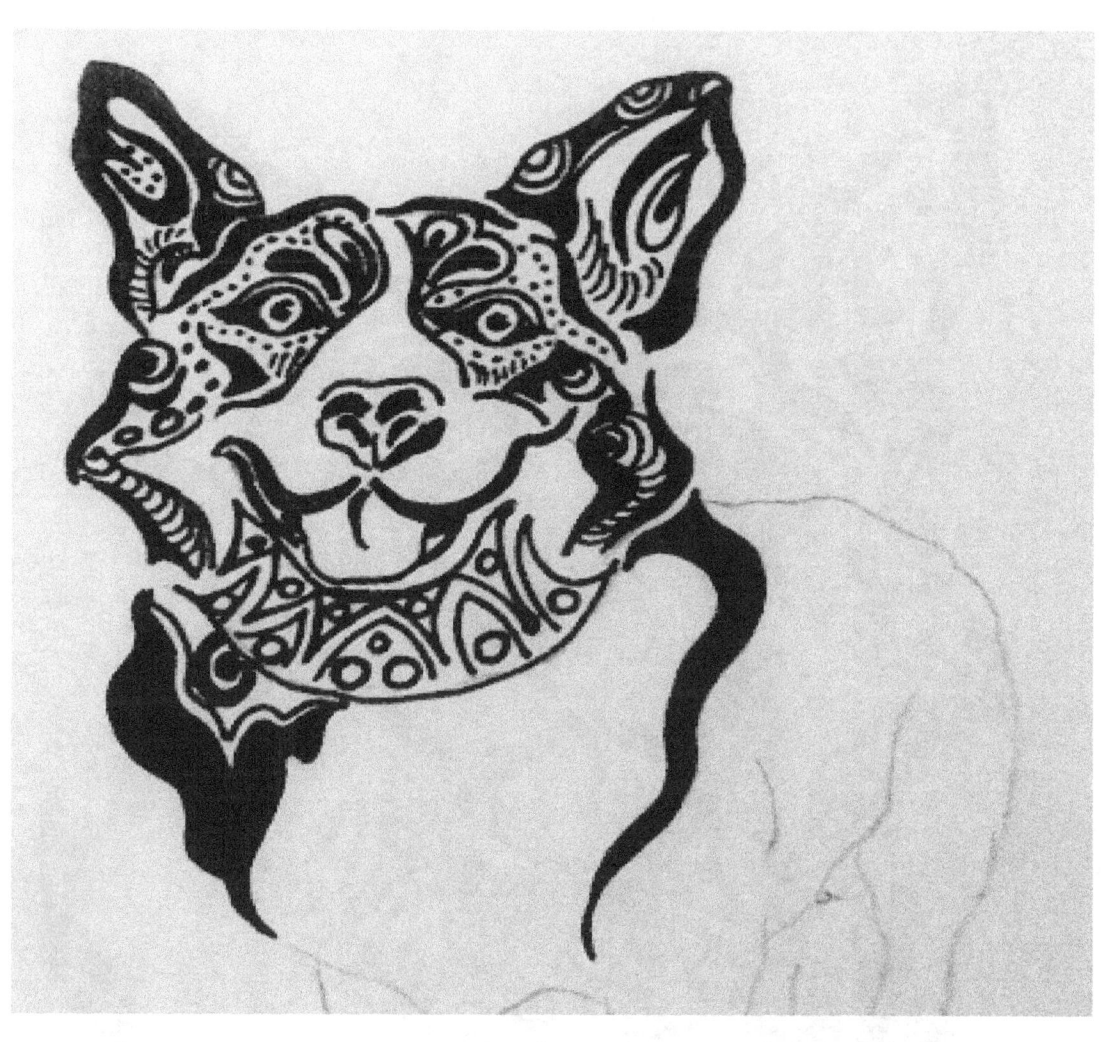

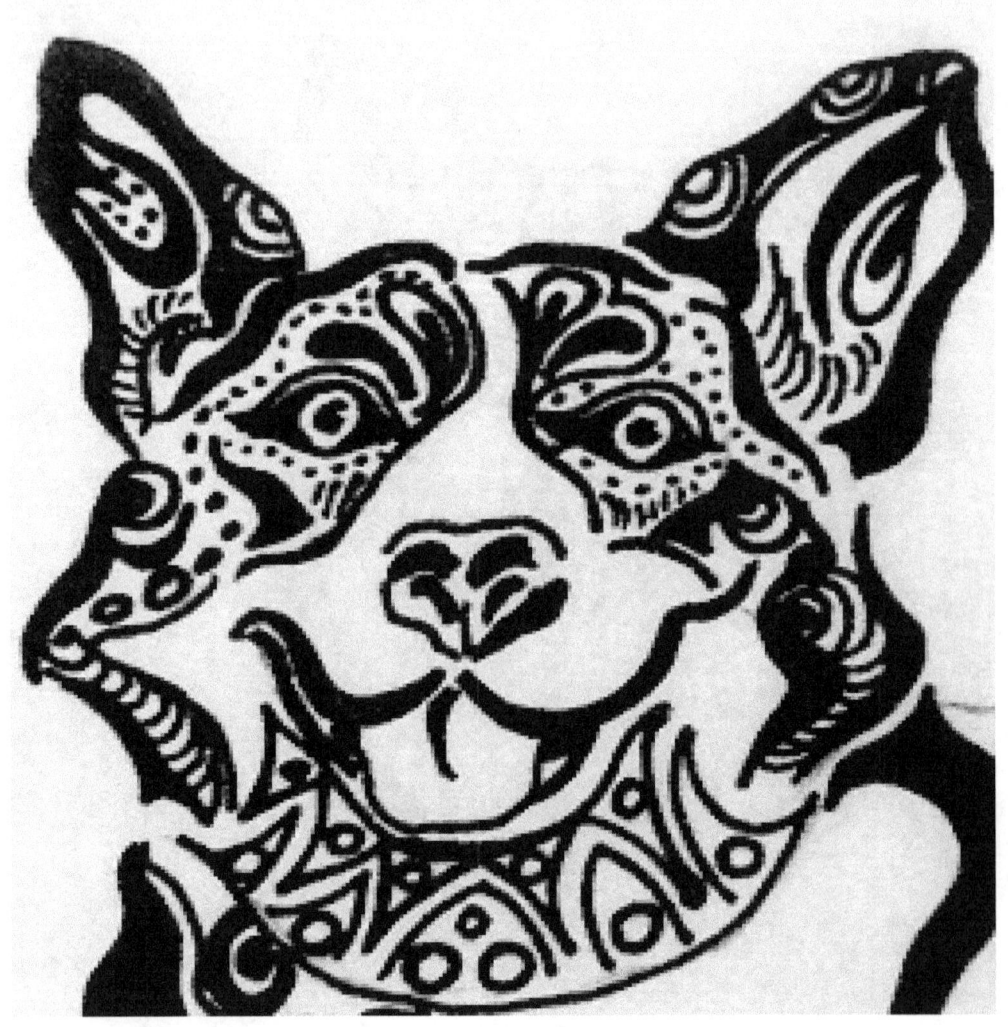

Add two bold, shaded regions extending on either side from the neck. On the right side, be sure to include the small, shaded circle and the unshaded region beneath it. Beneath the mouth, make a series of connected triangles with circles placed inside of each one. Beneath these triangles, make interconnecting triangles that also contain circular shapes.

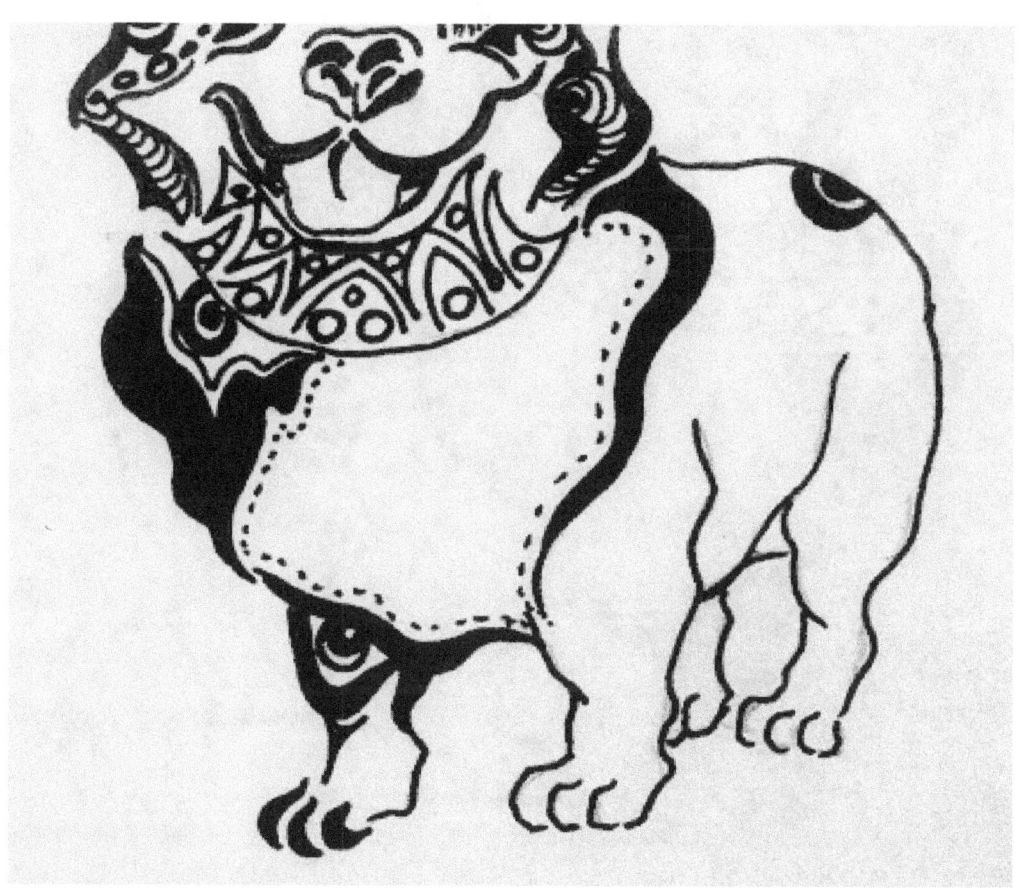

Make a dotted line around the chest region. Along the right, front leg make the shaded region shown in the drawing and the small concentric circles above it. Add some bold shading to the right front toes. On the back, make a small, bold semi-circle, ringed with a thick, shaded semi-circle.

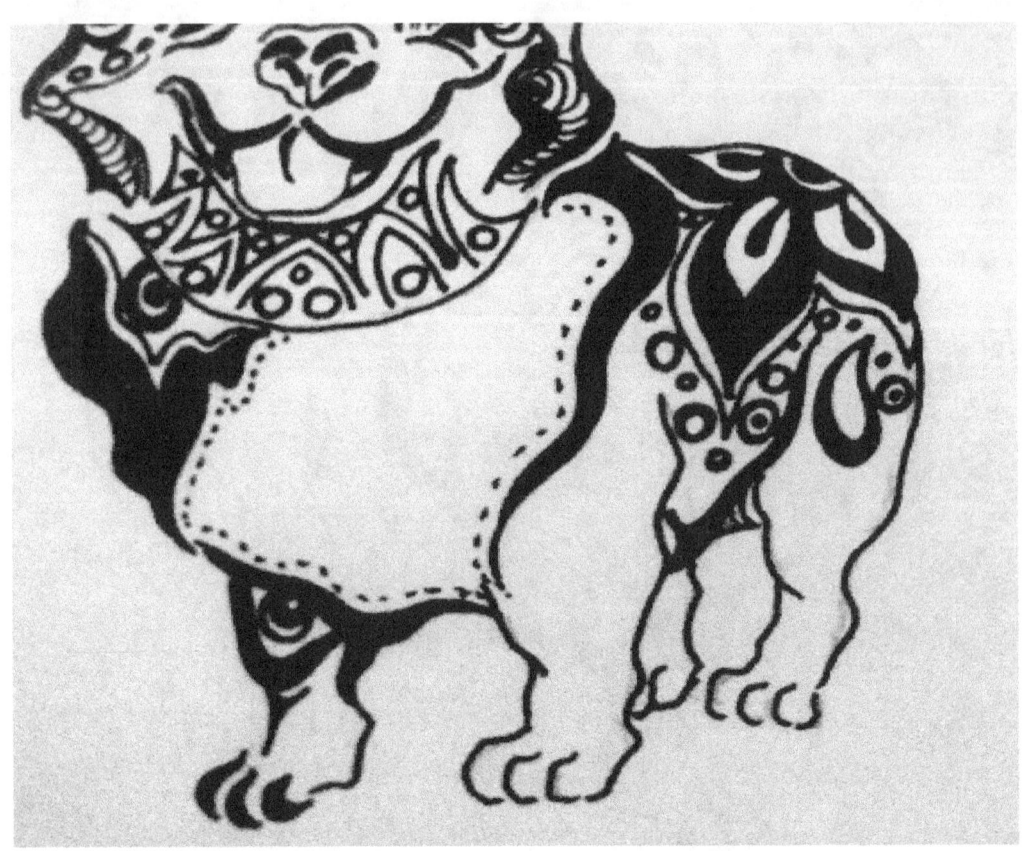

On the dog's back, make three large petal-like shapes extending from the circle you made on its back. Make alternate bands of shaded and unshaded regions in the petals and put another outline around the whole floral shape. Add several small circles along the bottom portion of the floral shape. Add a large paisley/teardrop shape on the rear leg with bold shading along its edges. Add a long, irregular diagonal shaded area between the rear legs.

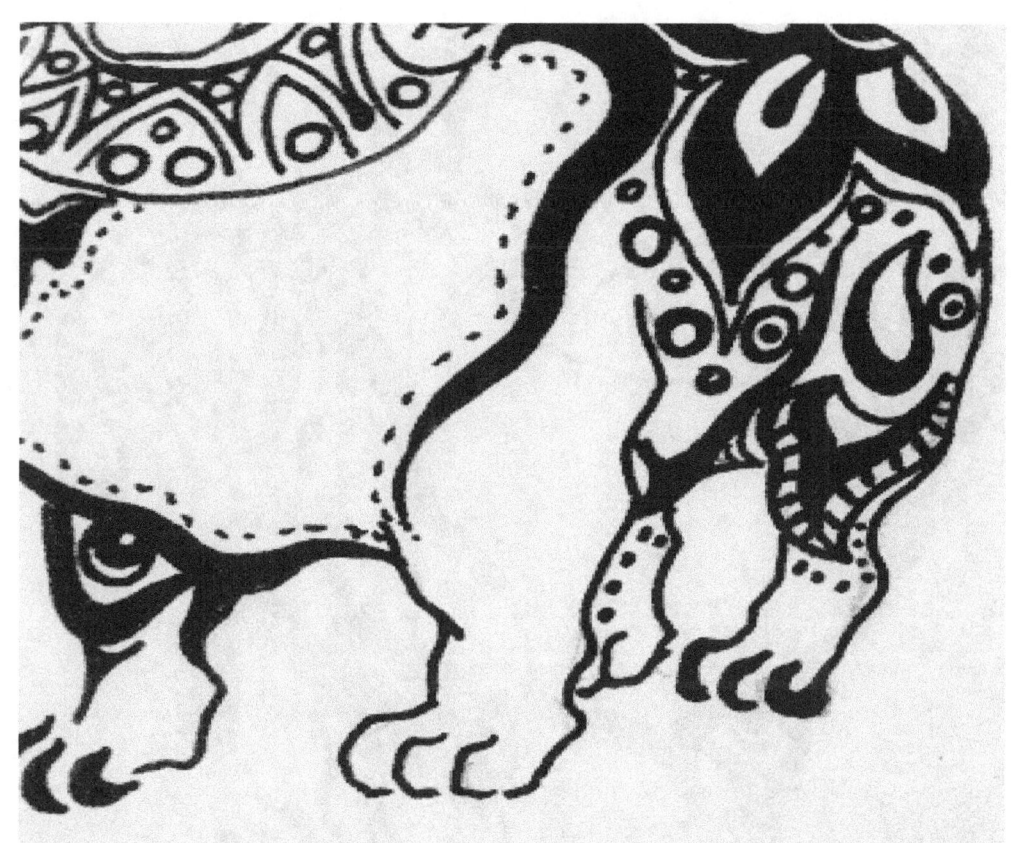

Add dotted lines along the rear legs and bold marks on the rear, left toes. Make a shaded, 'v' shaped region on the rear, left leg and outline it with dashed marks.

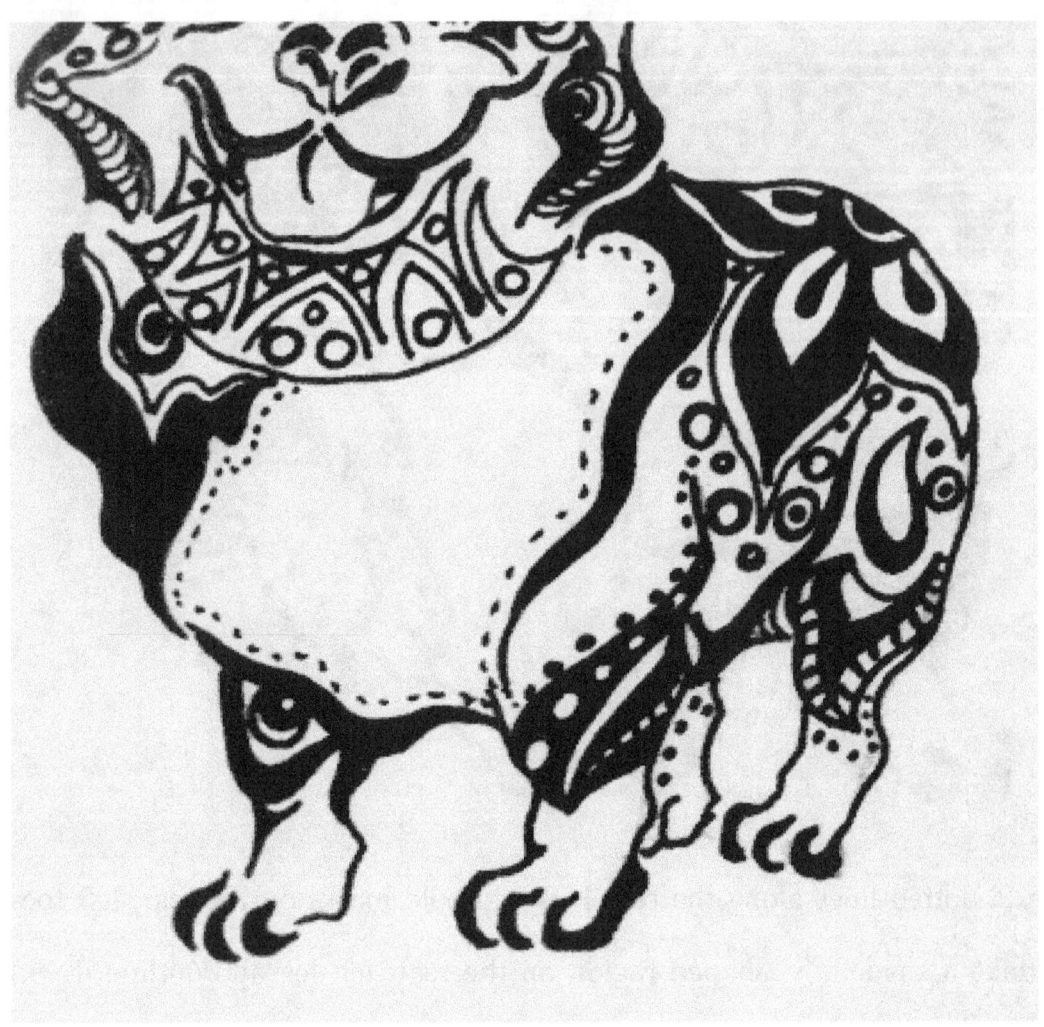

Add bold marks on the left, front toes. Make two long, road-shapes on the front, left leg and draw several small ovals inside of them. Shade in these shapes except for the ovals.

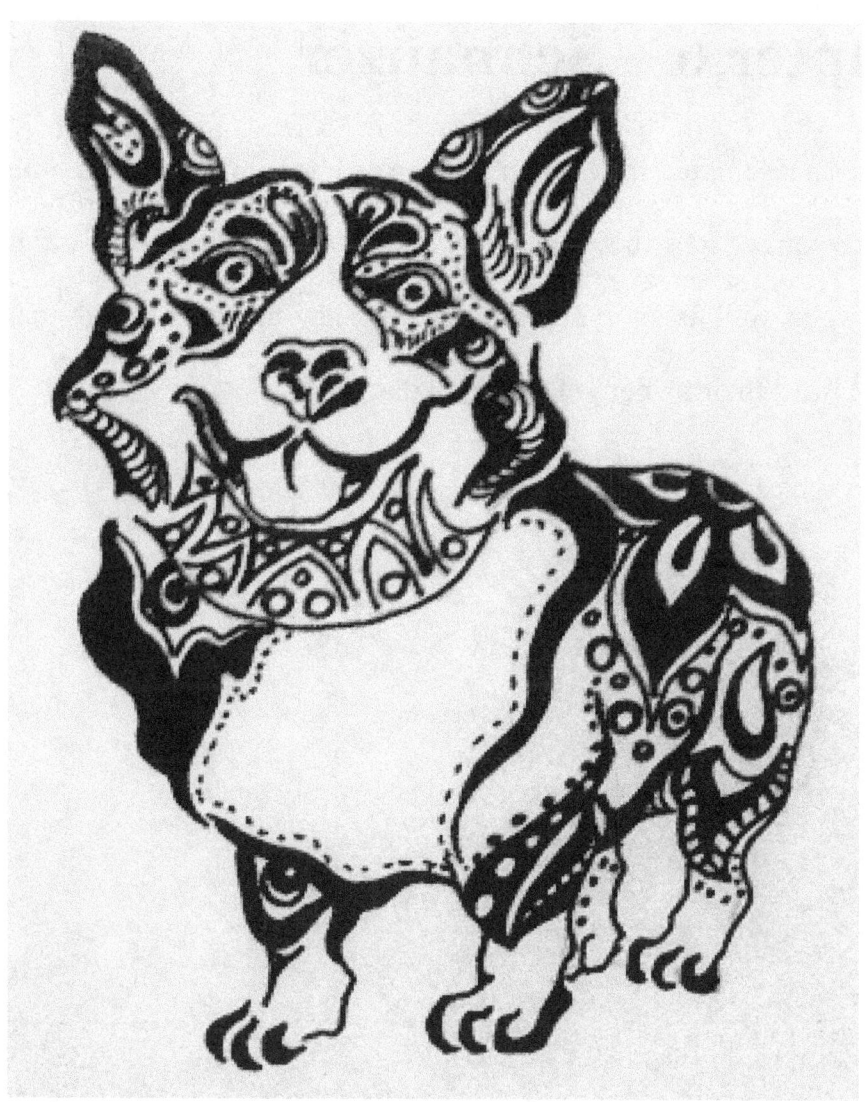

Now your corgi drawing is complete! Take a look at the completed drawing and see if there is anything you missed. Be sure to include any of these details.

Chapter 6 – Schnauzer

These dogs originated in Germany. The word 'schnauzer' means 'mustache'; and once you see how they look, you will know why. These dogs are friendly, protective as well as energetic and active. They make excellent guard dogs and will warn their owners of potential danger.

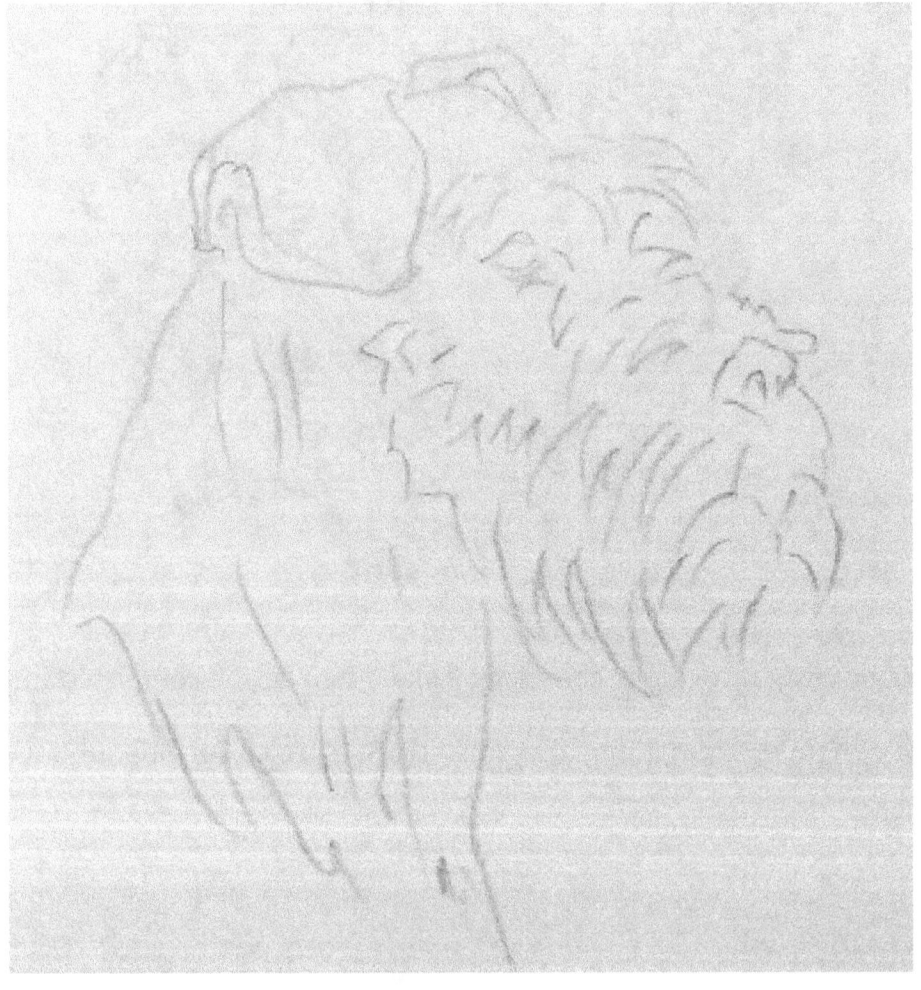

Make the outline of the dog's head and neck. Use several triangular strokes to make the animal's face. Draw the ears with a similar triangular shape.

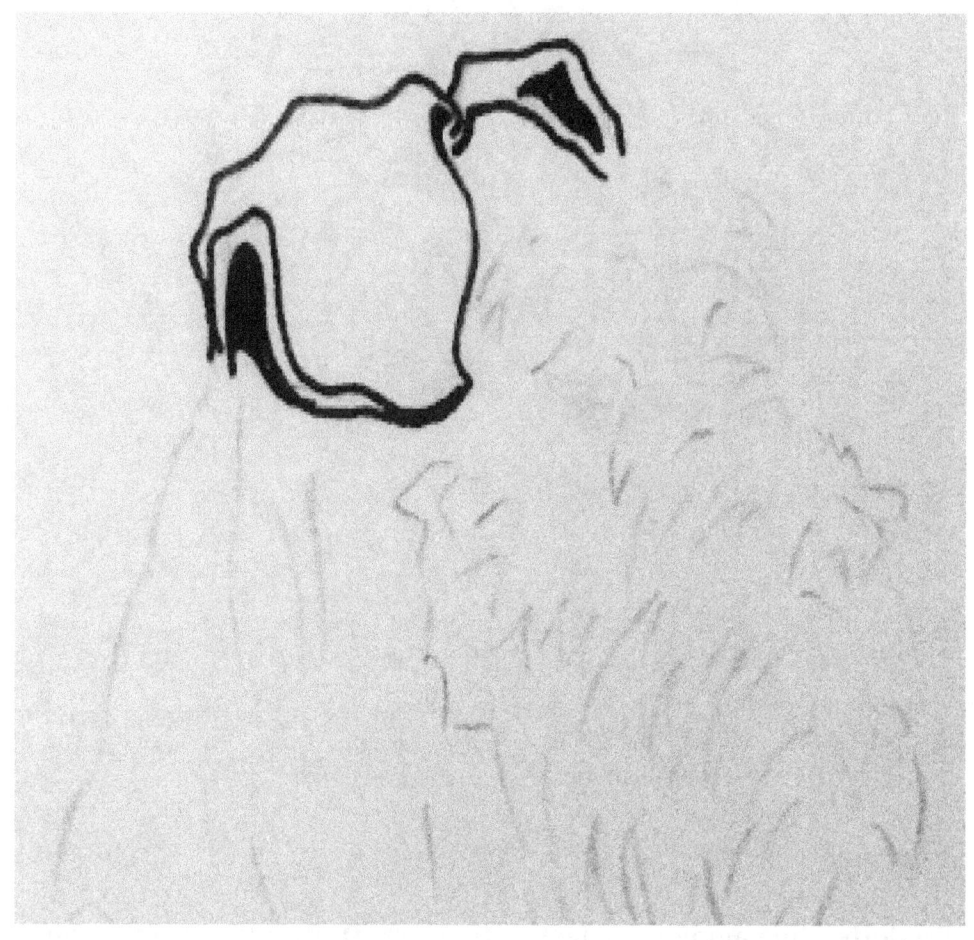

Go over the ears with dark markings. Make two regions that are shaded in completely as shown in the drawing.

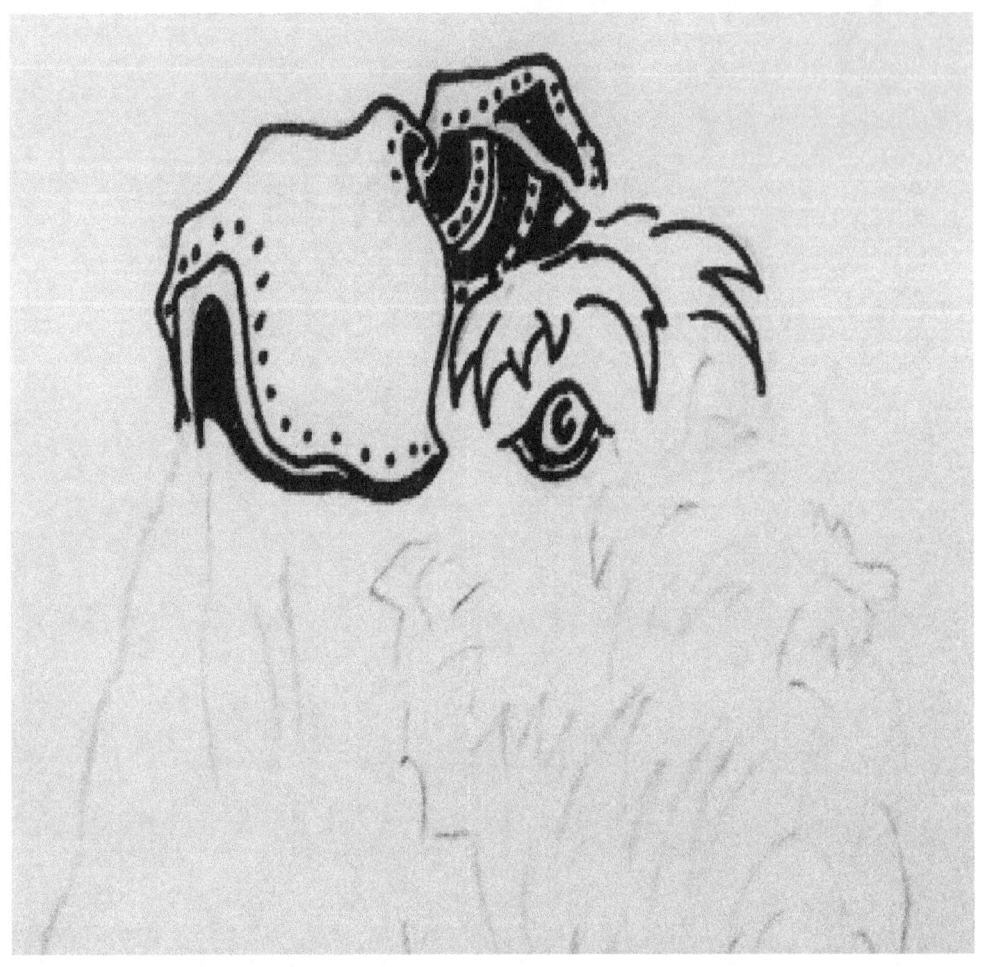

Draw a dotted line along the edges of the ears. Draw a couple of rectangular bands in between the ears and shade the region around it. Put a dotted line inside each of the bands. Go over the eyebrows and eye with dark markings. Inside of the eye, make a small shaded 'c' and shade in the area around the iris of the eye.

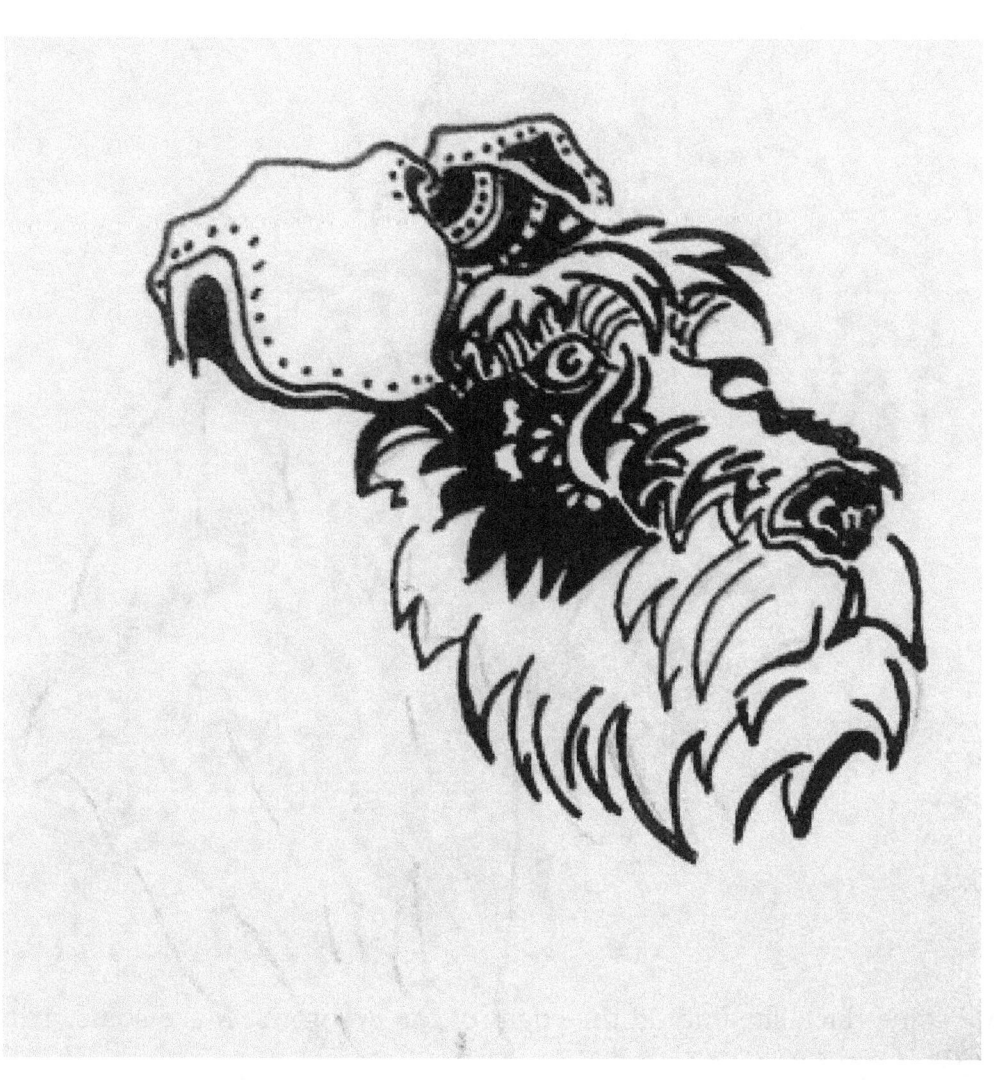

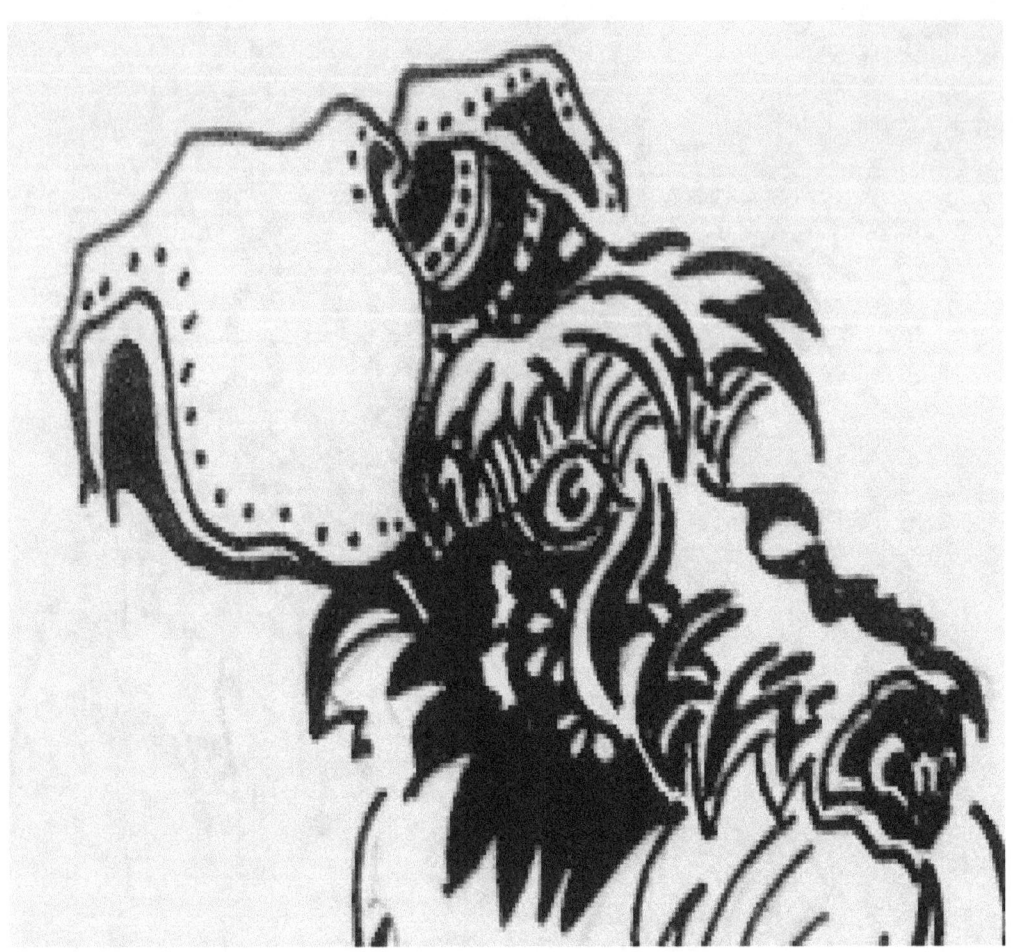

Add some thick shading on the edges of the eyebrows. Make some striped marks underneath the eyebrows. Make dark triangular marks long the bridge of the nose and along the snout and mouth. Underneath the eyes make a shaded region, leaving some small, petal-like shapes unshaded as shown in the drawing.

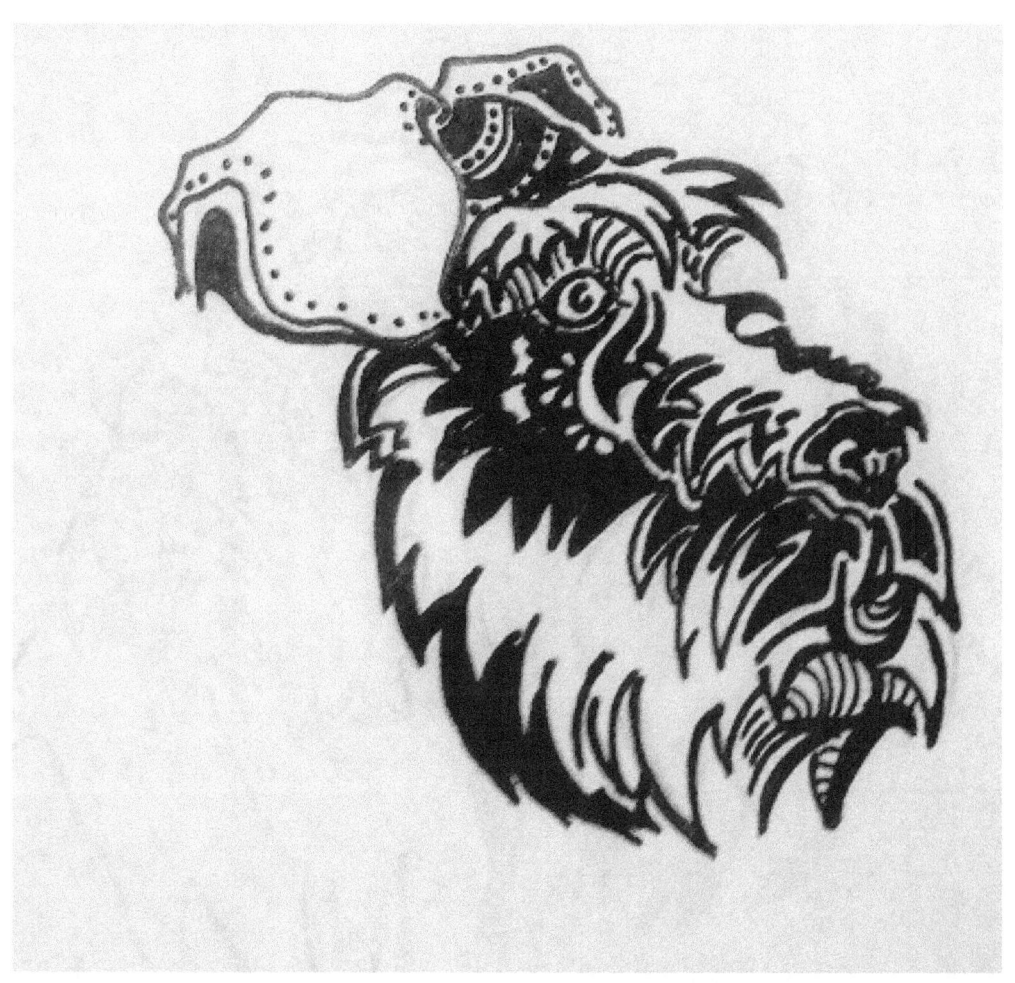

Continue the dark shaded region from beneath the eye all of the way to the snout. Add some dark shading along the lower left edge of the muzzle. Around the mouth region, make the concentric curved marks that you see in the drawing.

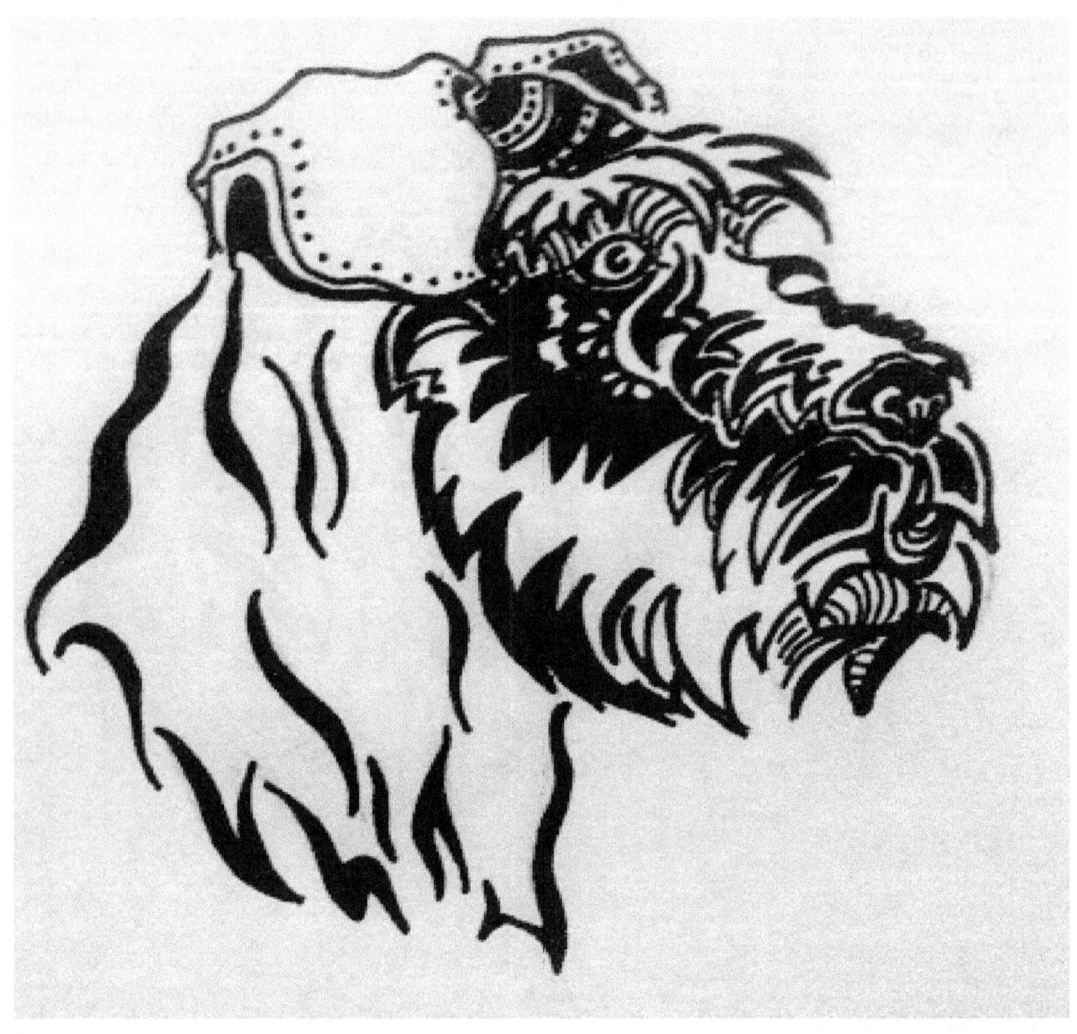

Draw in the thick, black curved marks that you see on the neck region.

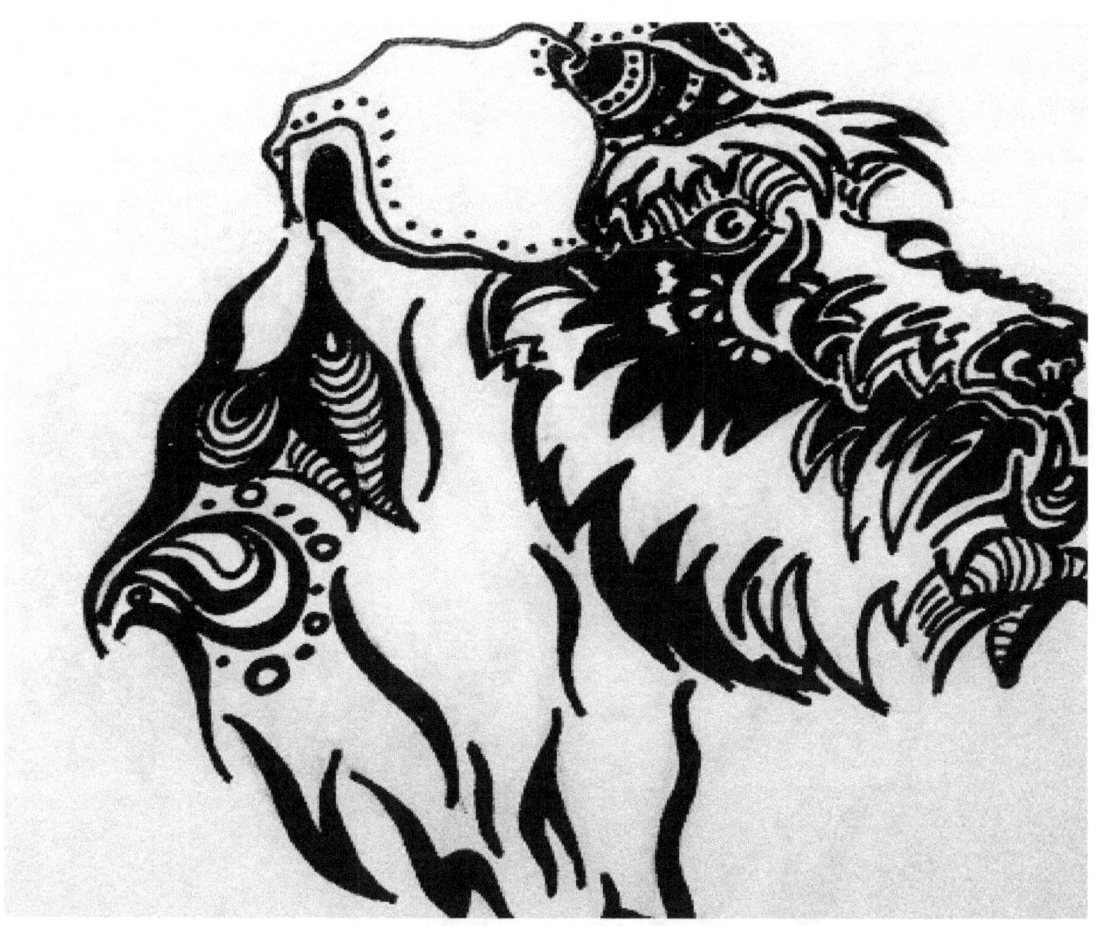

Make the three teardrop shapes that you see on the right side of the dog's head. Make the concentric circles that you see inside of the teardrops. Draw in the circular marks you see.

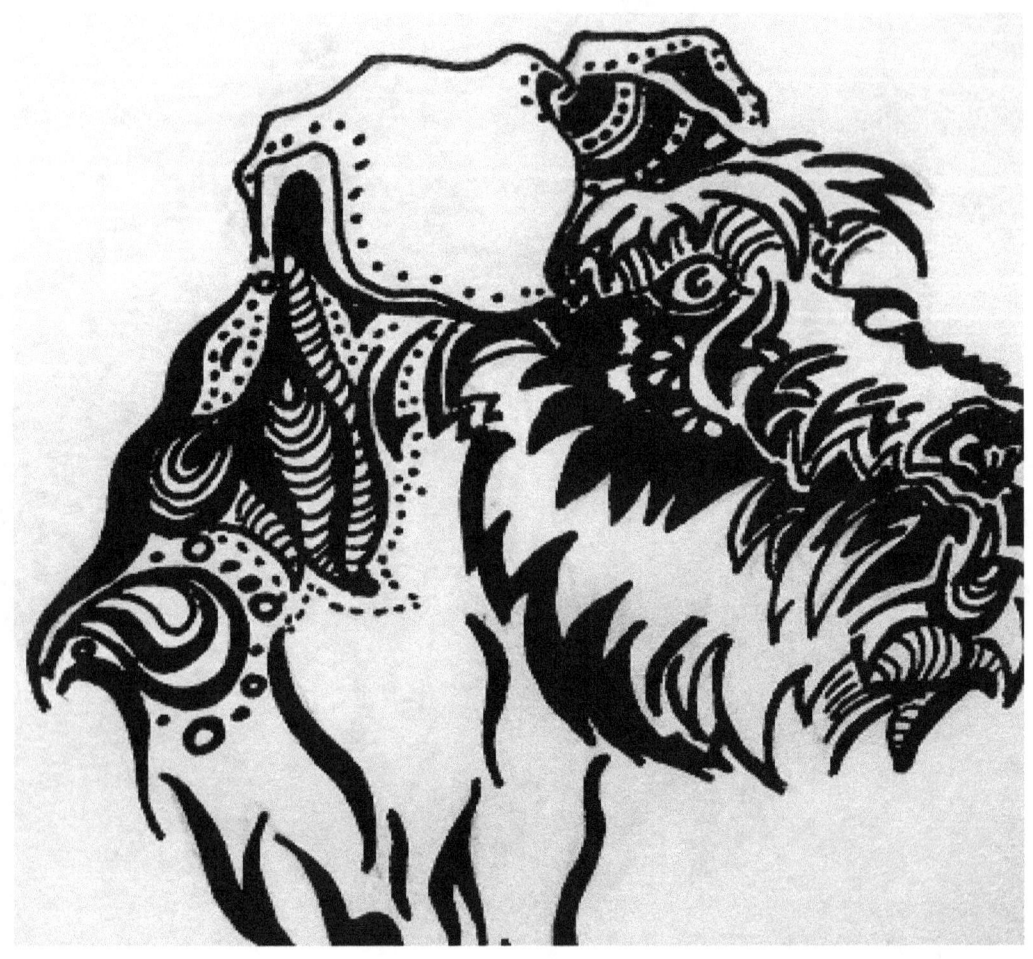

Add the dotted lines that surround the teardrops that you made. Add the

concentric marks that you see in the drawing beneath the ear.

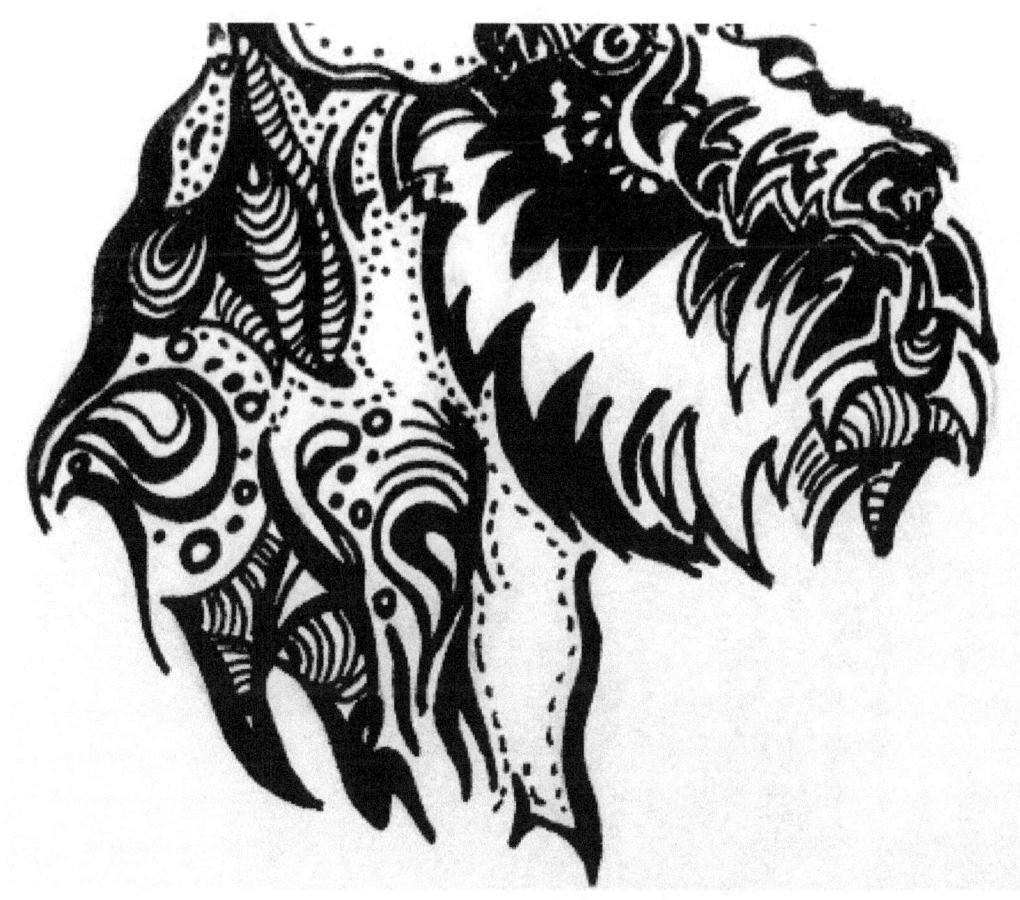

Inside the triangular shapes at the bottom of the drawing, draw in the concentric marks that you see. Above and to the right of this, make another teardrop shape and shade in the part in the middle, leaving an unshaded portion in the very center. Add in the additional dotted lines and circular marks shown in the drawing.

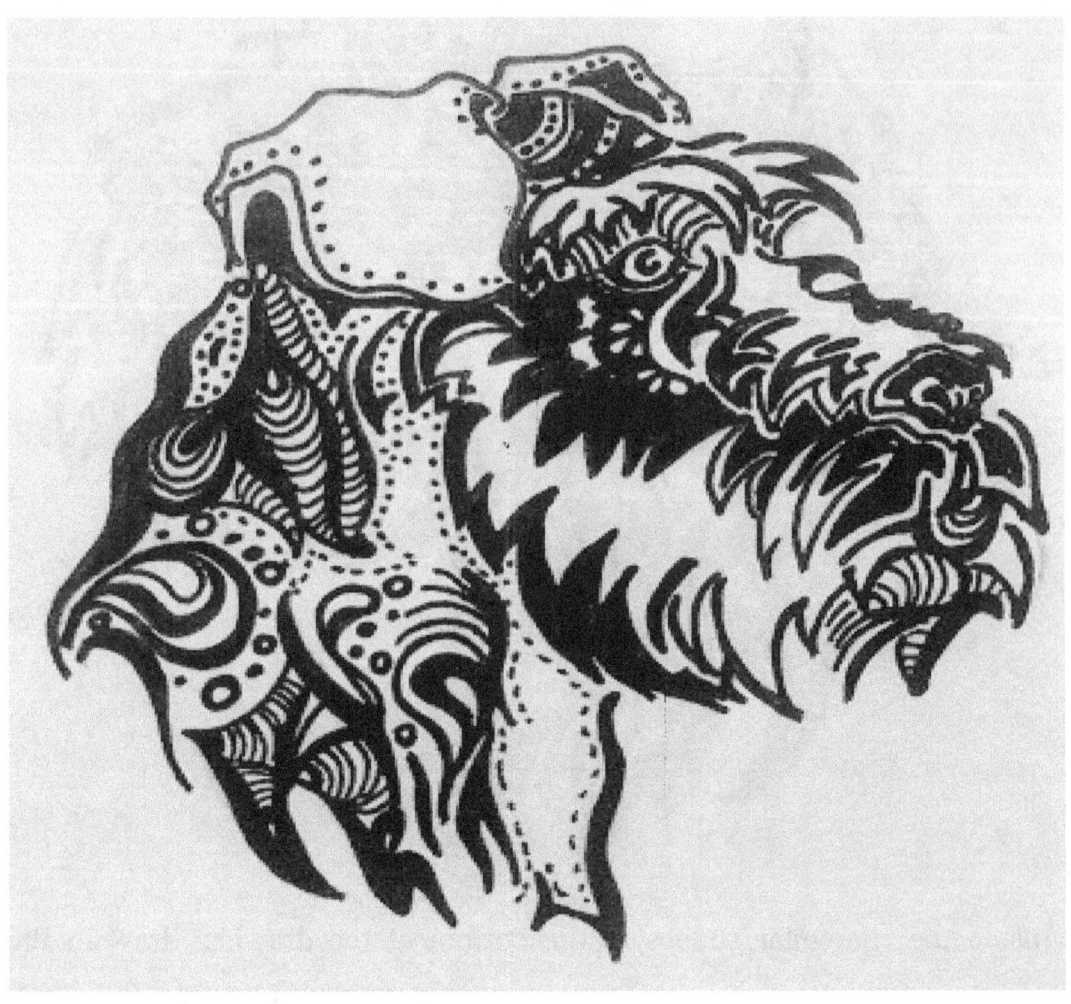

Here is the completed drawing of the schnauzer. Now is the time to go back and see if there are any details that you may have missed.

Conclusion

Dogs are wonderful companions and bring us so much joy. The various breeds of dogs all have their unique traits that endure them to us. They are also really fun to draw. We hope that you have become a more proficient illustrator and have become more skilled in the use of the Zen doodle method. Now, take what you've learned and make it your own. Draw a subject of your choice, possibly another breed of dog; and include the dark shading, floral designs, and concentric circular patterns that you have learned to use for these drawings. Hopefully this book has given you more tools for your toolbox as an artist as well as more of an appreciation for our four legged friends.

Thank you!

Thank you for choosing our book, we hope you found it interesting and helpful.

If you liked the book, please give us a favor to write your review here:

https://www.amazon.com/dp/B01B4BJYLE#nav-subnav

We would really appreciate this!

If you would like to have a bonus – **FREE BOOK**, please send the screenshot of your review to this:

lucy.artbooks@gmail.com

lucy.artbooks@gmail.com and we will send you a **FREE BOOK** in PDF as a **GIFT!****

Hope to see you in our future books and good luck in your drawing experience!

** in the e-mail subject please mention the name of the book you reviewed and the author.

www.ingramcontent.com/pod-product-compliance
Lightning Source LLC
Chambersburg PA
CBHW080716190526
45169CB00006B/2392